LAKE CHAMPLAIN
AS CENTURIES PASS

LAKE CHAMPLAIN
AS CENTURIES PASS

ALLEN PENFIELD BEACH

Basin Harbor Club
Basin Harbor, Vermont
and
The Lake Champlain Maritime Museum
Basin Harbor, Vermont

Copyright © 1994
Printed in the United States of America
First printing, June 1959
Second printing, April 1994
ISBN: 0-9641856-0-1

Cover:
"Bason Harbour Lake Champlain," c.1810
by Archibald Robertson

CONTENTS

PREFACE   *vi*

CHAPTER

I	In the Beginning	1
II	Indian Occupation of the Champlain Valley	7
III	Samuel de Champlain's Explorations	11
IV	French, Dutch, and English Strive for Control of the Champlain Valley	23
V	Contest Continues for Ownership of the Shores of Lake Champlain	37
VI	Capture of Fort Ticonderoga and the Revolutionary War	45
VII	Township of Ferrisburg	61
VIII	War of 1812	71
IX	Ferry and Steamboat Service on Lake Champlain	77
X	Recent Events Taking Place in the Champlain Valley, and its Many Attractions	95

Chronology of Important Dates   99

Bibliography   105

AFTERWORD   107

PREFACE

When our grandfather, Allen Penfield Beach, was a youngster growing up on the shores of Lake Champlain, life was a lot simpler than it is now. As a boy he hunted for arrowheads on her stream banks; later, as handyman extraordinaire at the fledgling resort at Basin Harbor, he farmed with a horse drawn plow. Water was pumped by windmill, or, on windless days, by a bull-powered treadmill.

Allen Penfield Beach

By the time he wrote this book, A. P. Beach had seen a lot of changes on the lake. The grand steamboats which carried nearly all the resort's supplies had been replaced by rail and car. The modern age brought the necessary conveniences of electricity and running water, as well as the luxuries of a golf course, swimming pool, and airstrip.

One thing the years did not change was our grandfather's love of Lake Champlain. He viewed it as a wealth of beauty and history that people should know about and enjoy. In fact, he was one of the earliest promoters of tourism in Vermont. He published the first issue of Vermont Life at his own expense. Although he recognized the lake's potential as a tourist attraction, A.P. Beach was a conservationist who felt that development was appropriate but must be done responsibly. He left much of his land holdings undeveloped; the buildings he did construct were situated with a careful regard to space and aesthetics. A self-taught architect, A.P. Beach employed classical design elements in the construction of the cottages he built for the resort. Whenever possible he used native materials, such as Vermont marble.

Our grandfather's love of Lake Champlain and his desire

to increase people's knowledge and understanding of its history and culture inspired him to write <u>Lake Champlain: As Centuries Pass</u> in 1959. The same love and desire has inspired us to republish it today. Although we have included illustrations, we have chosen not to edit his words at all. Readers should keep in mind, however, that some of his musings reflect a 1959 perspective. With the passage of time, for example, we have learned that it is better not to disturb archaeological sites both on land and under water, in order to preserve these resources for future generations.

The Beach family strives to build on A.P. Beach's legacy of lake education and preservation in other ways. Bob is co-founder and president of the Lake Champlain Maritime Museum, which serves to promote and preserve the history of Lake Champlain by documenting shipwrecks; building replicas; and spreading the word about the crucial role played by the lake in the birth of this country.

A.P. Beach was a man of vision and energy—and he had a passion for Lake Champlain. Like anyone with a passion, he didn't let things stand in the way of his goals. He was always looking for innovations, and when he traveled, he took copious notes on historical anecdotes, marketing schemes and better building techniques.

Were he alive today, we are certain our grandfather would be a strong voice for clean-up of the lake. More than most people in his day, he recognized that the lake is more than just a resource: it's a natural treasure that must be protected by all if it is to be enjoyed by any. It is our hope that the republishing of A.P. Beach's book will enhance people's understanding and appreciation of that treasure.

Bob and Penny Beach

1

In The Beginning

THE EARLY GEOLOGICAL HISTORY of the Champlain Valley is embedded in the indented rocky shores of the lake, in the countless fossils found in these rock formations, in the carved out harbors, in the boulders scattered over the area, in the glacial scratches on the exposed bed rock and the sandy beach at the foothills of the Green Mountains. More details of the story can be found in the marble, slate and granite quarries adjacent to the Champlain Valley. Students of geology can read the story like a book. It is an old story, not to be measured in centuries, but rather to be computed in millions of years, eons of time, somewhat beyond our comprehension.

    The records show that this entire area was once much lower than at the present time, with the ocean extending all through this valley and the Hudson River area, way up into Canada and the St. Lawrence River valley. During this era all of New England and a part of Canada was a very large island, possibly it might be called another continent. The ocean at that time extended back to the Green Mountains. During an even earlier period in the geological history when the rocky shores and mountain were formed, the climate was decidedly different from that at the present time. This is

Lake Champlain as the Centuries Pass

shown by the presence of fossils of tropical marine life found in the local rock formations. Some of the best examples are in a strata of rock on Button Island, which geologists have come from far and wide to study. This layer of rock scarcely two feet in thickness, contains an amazing variety of fossils including warm water sea corals and an endless collection of all forms of low animal life. There are a great many types of rocks to be found along the shores of Lake Champlain. There is black granite in the split rock range, sandstone and shale in certain areas; marble can be found on Isle LaMotte and at Mallett's Bay, red rocks in the Burlington area, but one of the most predominant rocks in the whole valley is known as Chazy limestone. Limestone in the Champlain Valley has its origin in the fragments of seashells, coral formations, bones, and teeth of fishes or skeletons of all sorts of sea life. These are mixed with lime muds, all of which are ground and blended together. This type of rock is of great interest to geologists since it contains an amazing amount of fossils portraying the history of the past, having more fossils than any other rocky formation. Walking along the shores between Basin Harbor and Button Bay one cannot help but

Fossils from the area reflect on an earlier era.

In the Beginning

notice the many fossils in the rocks. The most common kind is known as the Gastropods. These look very much like petrified snails and can be found in endless sizes. There will also be found tails of lizards, snakes and all sorts of other animal life which once thrived in this area. Limestone rock in itself is largely calcium carbonate and its chemical construction is not unlike that of the marbles. In fact, much of the limestone in the Champlain Valley can be finished similar to marble and it is quite dark when polished.

At the end of Split Rock Mountains is an entirely different rock formation than is found at any other point along the lake. Here the rocks are convoluted in twists and turns and folds that show what immense force was used to produce this rocky formation. The fact that this rock appears at this particular point is caused by a fault in the rock which caused this to slip up farther than the adjoining rock.

The geological events which had the greatest effect on the shaping of our scenery in the Champlain Valley were the many glacial periods which occurred no one knows how many hundred million years ago. Even the most recent ice age is said to have come about one hundred thousand years ago.

Split Rock Point.

Lake Champlain as the Centuries Pass

The magnitude of the glaciers and the force that they exerted is largely responsible for all of the many coves, harbors, and deep bays that line both shores of Lake Champlain. Not only did the glacier carve and gouge out the many harbors but it rounded off the tops of both the Green and the Adirondack Mountains and gave them their undulating contours which do so much to produce a pleasing landscape.

These glaciers were supposed to be upwards of ten thousand feet in thickness and as they passed down from Canada over the northern part of the valley, they had an action not unlike that of the giant road scraper spread across the valley. As they travelled along, they picked up all sorts of rocks and gravel from places to the northward and by the use of these boulders as tools similar to the chisels of a sculptor, the glacier carved out and scraped away everything that came in its path which was softer than the degree of hardness of the tools which it carried.

Wherever flat, bed rock surface is exposed, one may observe the gouged marks and scratches made by the southward moving glacier. The rounded tops of our mountains and the many hills and valleys which are prevalent on both sides of the lake are very definitely a result of the glacial action.

Studies made to determine the cause of the glacial periods and ice caps have come up with various theories. Naturally there was a change in the climatic conditions of the area to cause these ice ages. It might have been a shift in the earth's poles or that something happened to the solar system which supplied heat to the earth. It also might have been caused by the variation in the internal heat of the earth and the dissipation of the solar heat to various parts of the earth. However, we must give credit to the glacier for shaping the varied scenery of the Lake Champlain Valley.

Ellis W. Schuler, in his fascinating book entitled The Rocks

In the Beginning

and River, states "the lakes are the mirrors of the landscape. They hold together the beauty of the earth in the sky." This is certainly true of Lake Champlain which mirrors the mountains and its indented woodland shores.

How long it took for the climatic conditions to change, and the ice to melt away, is not known. It might have been ten or fifteen thousand years. However, the ice age disappeared eventually and, when the ice melted it produced a great deal of water which formed our lake. The lake was at first salt, as a result of its having been an arm of the ocean but the salt gradually disappeared and we now have a wonderful fresh water lake.

One of the most interesting geological features of the Champlain Valley is located on the New York side about one mile west of Port Kent. Here an amazing gorge of scenic and scientific interest has been cut through deep layers of Potsdam sandstone rock by the swift and dark waters of Ausable River. The chasm is about two miles in length and varies in width from ten to fifty feet. The depth is upward of two hundred feet. Many lateral fissures, narrow and deep, project from the main gorge making it an extremely fascinating place to visit. No one knows how many eons of time has taken for the river to gouge and carve the Ausable Chasm down to its present depth. However, the process is still going on.

2

Indian Occupation of Champlain Valley

MANY CENTURIES BEFORE any white man is known to have traversed the broad expanses of the body of water which we now call Lake Champlain, Indian tribes of many nations are known to have passed and repassed our shores in their frail, birch-bark canoes. They were either on the war path against hostile tribes, or were seeking out new hunting and trapping grounds for which the section was famous. Perhaps they came to the area to secure flint for making various implements of war. This body of water was the great thoroughfare for travel. Its channel led straight into the heart of the great North country. With short portages to the south, access was gained to Lake George and the Hudson River and then on to the Mohawk River and the central part of New York State. Following Otter Creek, to which the Indians gave the name "Pecunktuk," meaning Crooked River, they could travel by water most of the way into southern New England. The Indians had a full realization of the importance of the waterway as is indicated by the name they gave it "Caniadare Guarante," which in the Indian language meant "The Lake which is the Gate of the Country." A very early map also calls the lake The Sea of the Iroquois.

Lake Champlain as the Centuries Pass

Reggio was another Indian name applied to the Lake, mostly to honor a famous Mohawk Indian Chief who was drowned at Split Rock, four miles north of Basin Harbor, when the canoe in which he was traveling capsized in the rough water so often encountered when rounding this point. After this tragedy, the Indians handed down a legend that his spirit dwelt on the Point and controlled the winds and waves, and that a safe journey could be assured by casting trinkets overboard–thus paying homage to the spirit of the Indian warrior. The tradition seemed to have such a basis of fact that some attempts have been made to explore the bottom of the lake for Indian relics, but the water is too deep for amateur divers.

About 1740 the Dutch magistrate, Van Corlear, was traveling up to Split Rock from Albany on a scouting expedition. The story is that he scoffed at the Indian spirit as his boat passed the Point and suddenly the waves capsized his boat and he was drowned. So don't thumb your nose at the Indian spirit when you enter broad lake at Split Rock.

The late Mr. Truax of St. Albans, Vermont was considered one of the leading authorities on Indian lore, and he picked up with his own hands an amazing collection of Indian relics; he once told me that he had discovered camp site evidence which would indicate that some ten thousand Indians had been assembled near St. Albans Bay at various times. It was his opinion that the Indians had come there to secure a special sort of flint rock used in making arrow or spear heads. They also came to quarry flint at Mt. Independence, opposite Ticonderoga, where a fine grade of black flint was in abundance. At a much later date, this was a source of musket flints used by colonial troops.

Evidences of Indian occupation are to be found at countless places along the shores of the lake and particularly along the banks of the rivers emptying into the lake. The steams provided good fishing and trapping as well as safe

Indian Occupation of the Champlain Valley

passage for their canoes in any weather. When thus located, they were out of sight of migratory unfriendly tribes that might be traveling the lake.

Several fine collections of Indian relics consisting of arrowheads, stone axes, scalping knives, and stone and clay pottery, have been picked up locally along the banks of Otter Creek, Little Otter and Dead Creek. The late Judge Barnes who enjoyed a lifetime residence at Chimney Point (Scalp Point), twelve miles south of Basin Harbor, assembled a most interesting assortment of such specimens, all of which he found on his own property.

The Fleming Museum in Burlington has some rare Indian relics obtained by Dr. Perkins, and the collection assembled at Fort Ticonderoga by the Pell family is particularly noteworthy.

Some fifteen miles south of Basin Harbor there is another quarry site where Indians evidently gathered and set up an arrow-head workshop. Flint suitable for making arrow-heads had definite cleavage characteristics and the Indians used a sort of stone anvil and hammer stone to rough out the weapons. Many of these anvils and hammer stones have

This perfect half of an indian pot was found in 20 feet of water off a lake island in 1988 by Duncan and Sandra Steeves. It is now on exhibit at the Lake Champlain Maritime Museum.

Lake Champlain as the Centuries Pass

been found at local Indian Camp sites. It is amazing to see what fine symmetrical arrow-heads were turned out with these crude tools. To the north in the deep bay beyond Long Point called by the French "Bay des Varseaux," the writer has frequently picked up arrow-heads and on one occasion, a beautiful stone axe.

One might naturally think that everything of this nature has already been discovered; however, new material is constantly coming to light. Recent excavation along the shores of Dead Creek near Lovers' Lane on the Vergennes-Basin Harbor road, have yielded some entirely new types of archaic material. One camp site was found at a depth of several feet, another fairly near the surface, indicating that considerable time had elapsed between the two occupations and that a flood had occurred in the interim. A basket containing a baby's skeleton was uncovered at this site.

A large Indian burying ground of an archaic culture estimated to be five thousand years old, has been recently discovered on East Creek, opposite Fort Ticonderoga by Mr. Olsen of the American Indian Museum of New York City. This has come to be known as the Folsom Village of "Red Paint People" and antedates all previous records of Indian occupation in the Champlain Valley.

It is therefore seemingly impossible to determine how many centuries of Indian occupation there were previous to the coming of Samuel de Champlain's expedition in 1609. The shores of some of our streams and lakes are still like unopened pages of history waiting to be read.

3

Samuel de Champlain- Explorations

Details of the Discovery of the Lake Champlain

CHAMPLAIN WAS BORN in the town of Brouage, France in the year 1567, son of naval captain Antoine Champlain and his wife Marguerite. The town of Brouage is no longer on the sea coast, as the once busy harbor has been filled in and the site of his birth is now known as Chareute Inferieure, a neglected hamlet ten miles inland from Rochefort on the Bay of Biscay. Exhaustive research has failed to establish the exact date of his birth, though the home site has been identified and a stone archway from the garden adjoining the home has been brought to Canada and is on display at the Chateau du Ramsay in Montreal. The small seaport town where he was born was famous for hardy sailors and his early life was spent mostly on the sea. His was an age of exploration and he soon became a true Viking "who loved the toss of waves and the howling of winds in the shrouds." His strength and agility seemed inexhaustible. In the whole course of French history, there are few personages as fascinating as Samuel de Champlain.

It is obvious that he came from a good family and had received a liberal education. Compared with many contemporary explorers, Champlain stands above them all in the range of his achievements. In addition to being a natural

Lake Champlain as the Centuries Pass

leader and an untiring traveler, he also acted as the historian of his expeditions and has left detailed descriptions that enable one to picture clearly the places he visited and the habits and living conditions of those with whom he came in contact. By 1588, Champlain was serving in the army of Henry of Navarre, King of France; however, he soon joined the navy. On his first voyage to America at the age of twenty-two he was in command of the ship "St. Julien," then under ownership of Spain.

The fleet left San Lucar in January, 1599 and Champlain visited the West Indies, Mexico, Cartegena and Isthmus of Panama and was the first man to point out the need of a canal at this point. This journey required two years and eight months. He made such a good report to Henry IV that the king gave him a pension and a patent of nobility so that he was thereafter known as Sieur de Champlain.

In 1603, Champlain accompanied a fur-trading expedition under the patronage of Aymer de Chastes, Governor of Dieppe, at which time they explored the St. Lawrence and learned from the Indians of great bodies of water on the interior, all of which Champlain visited in following years.

Governor Chastes died during Champlain's absence but Champlain found another sponsor in Sieur de Montes, a Huguenot noble of Champlain's own province. He started out again in 1605 and was the first explorer to make a detailed examination of the coast of New England and Nova Scotia and to prepare a full and accurate report of his observations. He was first to discover and name Mt. Desert Island in Maine. He explored the Charles River in Massachusetts fifteen years before the Pilgrims landed at Plymouth.

He reported a great many Indians in the area and though his sponsors had sent him to select a site to colonize with a more favorable climate than the St. Lawrence Valley, he apparently was not impressed with the New England Coast.

In 1608, Champlain attained the wish of his heart when he

SAMUEL DE CHAMPLAIN'S EXPLORATIONS

persuaded the king to permit him to establish a colony on the St. Lawrence at the present site of the City of Quebec. He sailed away in the ship "De Don de Dieu" leaving Honfleurs April 13 and reached Tadousac in the St. Lawrence June 3. A month was spent looking for a good site and on July 3 he arrived at Quebec and started workmen building permanent quarters for the first French colony in America.

He spent the winter there with twenty-eight companions and his description of their experiences makes interesting reading. He was completely sold on the new country. In his book of voyages he gives glowing accounts of the richness and beauty of the country, the unlimited amount of fish and game and the varied pleasures of living in New France. The following extracts from his writings could easily be employed by modern real estate developers:

> "Thus one can judge of the pleasure that the French will have when once they are settled in these places; living a sweet, quiet life, with perfect freedom to hunt, fish, and make homes for themselves according to their desires; with occupation for the mind in building, clearing the ground, working gardens, planting them, grafting, making nurseries, planting all kinds of grain, roots, vegetables, salad greens and other pot herbs, over as much land and in as great a quantity as they wish."

It had always been the policy of Champlain to keep on good terms with the Indians. In order to continue his explorations of the inland country he cultivated the friendship of the native tribes which at that period happened to be the Algonquins, Hurons and Ottawas. These tribes though larger than those of the Iroquois federation, were less intelligent and more barbarous.

However, it was these allies who marked out for Champlain the course of his journey to the Champlain Valley.

Lake Champlain as the Centuries Pass

When the young Indian chiefs visited Quebec, they were awed by the cannon and the distant effect wrought by their fire. They implored Champlain "to come with them and hurl his thunder and lightning at their enemies, the Iroquois, who inhabited the distant lake country." This suggestion suited Champlain's love of adventure and by June 28, 1609, he had an expedition fitted out to travel southward.

A large, well-equipped shallop was secured in which to make the journey, the Indians having told him that such a boat could pass the Iroquois River (Richelieu) rapids. He was quite disappointed to find passage of the rapids impossible. He decided, however, to continue on with his Indian cohorts by means of canoes which could be carried past the rapids. Only two of this white companions volunteered to make the hazardous trip with him, the balance of his men returning to Quebec with the shallop. He states in his records that twenty-four canoes were used to transport the party of sixty Indians and three white men on a journey that took them nearly the entire length of the lake.

These Indian canoes are described as "being about eight or nine paces long and about one and a half paces wide in the middle, diminishing at both ends. They are made of birch bark strengthened inside with little hoops of white cedar."

In describing the lake, Champlain says:

"The next day, (July 4th) we entered the lake, which is of great extent, perhaps fifty or sixty leagues. There I saw four beautiful islands. There are also several rivers that flow into the lake that are bordered by many fine trees, of the same sorts that we have in France, with a quantity of vines more beautiful than any that I had seen in any other place, . . . and many chestnut trees. There is a great abundance of fish of a good many varieties. Among other kinds is one called by the savages, Chaousarous, which is

SAMUEL DE CHAMPLAIN'S EXPLORATIONS

of various lengths, but the longest as these people told me is eight to ten feet. I saw some of them five feet long and as big as a man's thigh. The savages gave me the head of one of them. They set great store by them, saying that when they have a headache, they bleed themselves with the teeth of this fish where the pain is and it passes off at once."

Champlain relates a tall tale about the remarkable cunning of this fish.

"When it wishes to catch certain birds, it goes into the rushes or weeds which border the lake in certain places, and puts its snout out of the water without moving at all so that when the birds coming to light on its snout, thinking it is the trunk of a tree, the fish is so skillful in closing its snout which had been half open that it draws the bird under by its feet." This, he adds, is what people told him, which indicates the Indians of those days liked to make up a good story.

"Continuing our course in this lake, on the east side I saw as I was observing the country, some very high mountains with snow on top of them (Mt. Mansfield)." This was obviously an optical illusion due to a fog bank on the mountainside. "I saw on the south others (Adirondacks) not less high than the first but they had no snow at all."

Their progress down the lake was slow averaging only four or five miles a day. As they approached the vicinity of Basin Harbor, they did all their traveling by night and doubtless spent one or more days in this section. Champlain's description of the last days of the journey and the battle with the Iroquois is so complete in details that it seems worthy of a place in this short narrative.

Lake Champlain as the Centuries Pass

"As we began to approach within two or three days' journey of the home of the enemies, we did not advance any more except at night and by day we rested. Nevertheless, they did not omit at any time the practice of the customary superstitions to find out how much of the undertaking would succeed and they came to me to ask if I had dreamed and if I had seen their enemies. When night came we pursued our journey until daylight, when we withdrew into the thickest part of the woods and passed the rest of the day there.

"About ten or eleven o'clock, after having taken a little walk around our encampment, I went to rest; and I dreamed that I saw the Iroquois, our enemies, in the lake near a mountain, drowning within our sight and when I wished to help them our savage allies told me that we must let them all die and that they were worthless. When I woke up they did not fail to ask me, as is their custom, if I had dreamed anything. I told them the substance of what I had dreamed. This gave them so much faith that they no longer doubted that good was to befall them.

"When evening came, we embarked in our canoes to continue on our way and as we were going along very quietly and without making any noise on the twenty-ninth of the month (July) we met the Iroquois at the end of a cape that projects into the lake on the west side and they were coming to war. We both began to make loud cries, each getting his arms ready. We withdrew towards the water and the Iroquois went ashore and arranged their canoes in a line, and began to cut down trees with poor axes, which they sometimes get in war, and also with others of stone; and they barricaded themselves very well.

"Our men also passed the whole night with their canoes drawn up close together, fastened to poles, so that they might not get scattered, and might fight all together, if there were need of it; we were on the water within arrow range of the side where their barricades were.

Samuel de Champlain's Explorations

"When they were armed and in array, they sent out two canoes set apart from the others to learn from their enemies if they wanted to fight. They replied that they wanted nothing else; but that, at the moment there was not much light and that they must wait for daylight to recognize each other, and that as soon as the sun rose they would begin the battle. This was accepted by our men; and while we waited the whole night was passed in dances and in songs, as much on one side as on the other, with endless insults and other talk, such as the little courage they had, their feebleness and inability to make resistance against their arms and that when day came they should feel it to their ruin. Our men also were not lacking in retort, telling them that they should see such power of arms as never before, and much other talk, as is customary in siege of a city. After plenty of singing, dancing and parley with one another, daylight came. My companions and I remained concealed for fear that the enemy should see us, preparing our arms as best we could, separated however, each in one of the canoes of the Montagnais savages. After arming ourselves with our light armor, each of us took an arquebus and went ashore. I saw the enemy come out of their barricade, nearly two hundred men, strong and robust to look at, coming slowly towards us with a dignity and assurance that pleased me very much. At their head there were three chiefs. Our men also went forth in the same order, and they told me that those that wore three large plumes were the chiefs, and that there were only three of them and that they were recognizable by these plumes, which were a great deal larger than those of their companions; and that I should do all I could to kill them. I promised to do all in my power, and said that I was very sorry that they could not understand me well, so that I might give order and system to the attack of the enemy, in which case we should undoubtedly destroy them all; but this could not be remedied; that I was very glad to encourage them and to show them the good will that I felt, when we should engage in battle.

"As soon as we were ashore, they began to run about two hundred paces towards the enemy, who was standing firmly and had not yet noticed my companions, who went into the woods with some savages. Our men began to call me with loud cries, and to give me a passageway; they divided into two parts and put me at the head, where I marched about twenty paces in front of them until I was thirty paces from the enemy. They at once saw me and halted, looking at me, and I at them. When I saw them making a move to shoot at us, I rested my arquebus against my cheek and aimed directly at one of the chiefs. With the same shot, two of them fell to the ground, and one of their companions, also who was wounded and afterwards died. I put four balls into my arquebus. When our men saw this shot was so favorable to them, they began to make such loud cries that one could not have heard it thunder. Meanwhile, the arrows did not fail to fly from both sides. The Iroquois were much astonished that two men had been so quickly killed, although they were provided with armor woven from cotton thread and from wood, proof against their arrows. This alarmed them greatly. As I was loading again, one of my companions fired a shot from the woods which astonished them again to such a degree that seeing their chiefs dead they lost courage, took to flight and abandoned the field and their fort, fleeing into the depths of the woods. Pursuing them thither, I killed some more of them. Our savages also killed several of them and took ten or twelve of them prisoners. The rest escaped with the wounded. There were fifteen or sixteen of our men wounded by arrow shots, who were soon healed. After we had gained the victory, they amused themselves by taking great quantities of Indian corn and meal from their enemies and also their arms, which they had left in order to run better. And, having made good cheer, danced and sung, we

Samuel de Champlain's Explorations

returned three hours afterwards with the prisoners. This place where this charge was made is in latitude 43° and some minutes, and I named the lake Lake Champlain."

Samual de Champlain sketched the 1609 battle scene which took place on what was to be called Lake Champlain. By permission of the Houghton Library, Harvard University.

Historians have waged a dispute for decades regarding the location of this battle. Champlain states that it was "on a cape extending out into the lake." This would indicate Crown Point, this being the only place with a cape extending into the lake. Those who believe the battle was at Ticonderoga state that Champlain casually mentions going to another lake after the battle. This could only mean Lake George.

After the battle was over, the victors started northward and after going eight leagues, which would have brought them somewhere in the vicinity of Button Bay, they camped for the night and proceeded to torture one of the prisoners, greatly to the horror and disgust of Champlain. Let him describe the unbelievable scene.

Lake Champlain as the Centuries Pass

"After going eight leagues, towards evening they took one of the prisoners and harangued him about the cruelties that he and his people had inflicted on them, without having any consideration for them; and said that similarly he ought to make up his mind to receive as much. They commanded him to sing, if he had any courage; which he did, but it was a song very sad to hear.

Meanwhile, our men lighted a fire, and when it was blazing well, each took a brand and burned this poor wretch little by little, to make him suffer great torment. Sometimes they stopped and threw water on his back. Then they tore out his nails and put the fire on the ends of his fingers and on his privy member. Afterward they flayed the top of his head and dripped on top of it a kind of gum all hot; then they pierced his arms near the wrists and with sticks pulled the sinews, and tore them out by force; and when they saw that they could not get them, they cut them. This poor wretch uttered strange cries and I pitied him when I saw him treated in this way; and yet he showed such endurance that one would have said that, at times, he did not feel any pain.

They strongly urged me to take some fire and do as they were doing, but I explained to them that we did not use such cruelties at all and that we killed them at once and that if they wished me to fire a musket shot at him, I would do it gladly. They said no and that he would not feel any pain. I went away from them distressed to see so much cruelty as they were practicing upon his body. When they saw that I was not pleased at it, they called me and told me to fire a musket shot at him, which I did without his seeing it at all.

After he was dead, they were not satisfied for they opened his belly and threw his entrails into the lake; then they cut off his head, his arms and his legs, which they scattered in different directions and kept the scalp, which

Samuel de Champlain's Explorations

they had skinned off as they had done with all the others that they had killed in the battle.

They committed also another wickedness, which was to take the heart, which they had cut into several pieces and gave to a brother of his and others of his companions, who were prisoners, to eat. They put it into their mouths but would not swallow it. Some Algonquin savages, who were guarding them, made some of them spit it out and threw it into the water. This is how these people treat those they capture in war; and it would be better for them to die in fighting or to kill themselves on the spur of the moment, as there are many who do, rather that fall into the hands of their enemies. After this execution, we resumed our march to return with the rest of the prisoners who always went along singing without any hope of being better treated than the other. When we arrived at the rapids of the river of the Iroquois, the Algonquins returned to their country and also the Ochatequins with some of the prisoners. They were well pleased with what had taken place in the war, and that I had gone with them readily. So, we separated with great protestations of friendship and they asked me if I did not wish to go into their country to aid them always as a brother. I promised that I would do so and I returned with the Montagnais."

Champlain was never known to have made another trip to the lake which he honored above all others by giving it his name. This open alliance of the French and the Algonquin Indians and their defeat of the Iroquois in this battle was in later years to work to the great disadvantage of the French in their attempts to colonize the shores of Lake Champlain.

The next recorded visit to Lake Champlain was in 1642 when Father Joques, the famous Jesuit missionary, came down with an expedition which ran into trouble. The priest was captured and tortured on Cole's Island which is located

Lake Champlain as the Centuries Pass

near Camp Dudley, four miles south of Westport. Here the Indians were reported to have cut off his thumb with a clam shell. He eventually escaped and lived to make more attempts to take Christianity to the savages but he was finally captured again and killed by those he tried to help.

The French, the Dutch and the English Strive for Control of the Champlain Valley

IT IS DOUBTFUL whether Champlain fully realized the importance to France of his discovery of the lake that was to bear his name. Certainly he could not have had any conception of the strife which would follow for the next one hundred and fifty years. The story of the passage of countless numbers of war parties that traveled back and forth through the lake during the period of the French occupation of the Champlain Valley had been covered by many students of history, particularly by Dr. Francis Parkman and at a later date by Guy O. Coolidge. The latter's writings published by the Vermont Historical Society in 1938, list the events of the era in great detail year by year, so I will only attempt to set down a brief summary of them with the names of some of the leaders.

The men, money and material that went for naught, and the extreme hardships that were endured, as well as the volume of traffic on the lake, can only be comprehended by a study of the original records and documents.

French claim to the territory was based not only on Champlain's discovery but also on the fact that some seventy years before the coming of Champlain, explorer Jacques Cartier sailed down the St. Lawrence to Montreal and on

Lake Champlain as the Centuries Pass

returning to France, told about the wonderful country to the south which the Algonquins had described to him. The Indians pointed out the ease with which these lands could be reached by water. It thus appears that the Champlain Valley was brought to the attention of Europe at a very early period, earlier, in fact, than any other part of North America.

There were, however, others who wanted possession of the Champlain Valley. When Henry Hudson, an Englishman in the employ of the Dutch East India Company, sailed up the river that was to bear his name, just a few months after Champlain had departed, he in turn was told about the great country to the north. Not knowing or caring about France's claim to the area, Hudson took possession of the territory as far north as the St. Lawrence River in the name of the States General of Holland and gave it the name of New Netherlands. An old 17th Century map in the museum at Basin Harbor shows the extent of this claim.

Even before the French had started to move into the Champlain Valley, the Dutch were well established at Albany which was known by the Dutch as Fort Orange. They made several trips of exploration of Lake Champlain and gave it the name of Corlaer in honor of the popular Dutch Governor of Fort Orange, Arendt Corlaer. Before the Dutch had made any attempt to establish a foothold on our shores, the English had taken over their claims to all of this area. On September 3, 1664, the Dutch flag was hauled down and the English flag floated over the settlement and the name was changed from New Amsterdam to New York, and Fort Orange to Albany, in honor of the Duke of Albany. While this was to be the end of Dutch dominance in North America, they held on at Albany for some time and on March 26, 1690, just a hundred years before Platt Rogers was to settle at Basin Harbor, Capt. Jacobus de Warm was sent up to Chimney Point to establish an outpost and Capt. Schuyler set up camp at Otter Creek.

THE FRENCH, DUTCH, THE ENGLISH STRIVE

The French, however, were becoming more and more active on the lake and had made many raids on the Dutch settlements to the south. They were looking with anticipation towards settling this territory and already had a fort at the north end of the lake. It was the English, however, who were to carry on the fight with France for the control of the whole North country. England based her claim partly on the original Dutch title, and partly on the grounds that it was Iroquois territory, and this tribe had been British allies since 1683. Godfrey Dellius, a minister at Fort Orange, had plans for settlements on the lake in 1696 and his nephew, Lydius, did some fur trading with the Indians at Chimney Point; steps were also being taken for English settlements on the lake.

About 1688, the French were giving serious consideration to the construction of a fort at the south end of the lake which would serve to protect the proposed settlements from Indian attacks.

By the treaty of Utrecht, April 11, 1713, the French Crown expressly recognized the sovereignty of Great Britain over the disputed area. However, the title to the area was by no means definitely settled and it was obvious that there was to be endless argument and dispute over these lands for many decades. The southern boundary of New France was not well established; the English thought it was Split Rock, but the French had in mind the southern end of Lake Champlain. The French, however, were first to see the possibilities of the area with its natural water highway leading directly to the wonderful land which Champlain had described so eloquently on his only visit in 1609.

Just about this time the King of France started making grants or seigniories on both sides of Lake Champlain. In order to protect the proposed settlements, a French force of some thirty men came down the lake on August 19, 1730 and started to build a fort on the site at what is now Crown

Lake Champlain as the Centuries Pass

Point. An inscription on the old fort walls indicates that Michel D'Agneau led this force.

A few years later this was developed into quite a formidable stone fort called Fort St. Frederick named after Frederic de Maurepas, who was French Naval Minister at that time. These were the first steps towards what was thought might become a great colonization on the shores of Lake Champlain. In 1732, Monsieur Anger made a very accurate survey of the lake. With this map to work from, the shores of the lake were

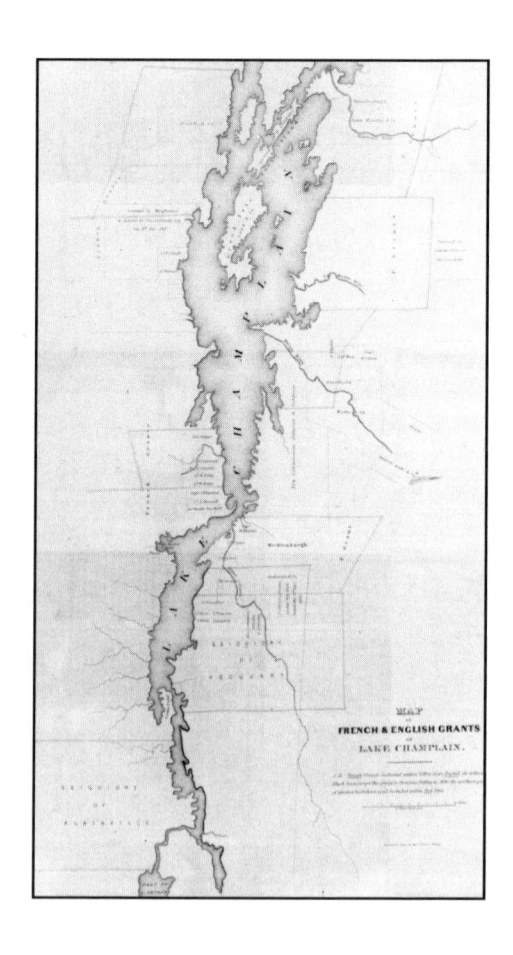

This "Map of French & English Grants on Lake Champlain" reflects the dynamic European effort to control the land surrounding the lake.

26

The French, Dutch, the English Strive

further divided into seigniories which were granted to favored individuals and military persons by the King of France. On July 7, 1734, the Basin Harbor area was granted to Sieurs Contrecour, Sr. and Jr. The grant to Sieurs Contrecour read "on the borders of Lake Champlain beginning at the mouth of the Riviere aux Loutres (Otter River) one league and half above and a league and a half below with a depth of two leagues together with so much of said Riviere aux Loutres as is found included therein with the three Islands or Islets which are in front of said concession and depend thereon."

On April 20, 1743, Gillis Hocquart, Entendant of Canada 1728-1748, received a large grant of land on the east shore of Lake Champlain from Louis, King of France. Hocquart wanted more land and secured another grant on April 1, 1745. The grant may have included as much as 115,000 acres.

After the French and Indian War, Gillis Hocquart, seeing the impossibility of holding his Lake Champlain grant, sold out his rights to Chartier de Lotbiniere for the sum of 9,000 livres. The value of the livre was about twenty cents. This is the first time that I found any record of cash having changed hands for Lake Champlain real estate. This was a shrewd deal on Hocquart's part, selling real estate which he had already lost. Lotbiniere made repeated efforts to get the British Government to recognize his title without avail.

It would appear from the records that a great many people were attracted to the shores of Lake Champlain and Anger's map shows the extent of the grants surveyed and put on record. In fact, nearly all of the land around the shores of the lake was given up at that time.

Up to the present time, I have been unable to find out the names of the people who settled along the shores of Lake Champlain during the brief period of French colonization. The fact remains, however, that there was a fairly large population established along the shores of the lake,

Lake Champlain as the Centuries Pass

particularly between Crown Point and Otter Creek; with the French stronghold at Fort St. Frederic, the settlement progressed rapidly. The point opposite the fort which we call Chimney Point appears on the old French maps as Point a la Chevelure (Scalp Point). Settlements were made here about the same time or shortly after the fort was established and a combined fort and windmill was constructed on the site of the old tavern. The location of this fort on the east side of the lake enabled the settlers to look up the lake whence hostile attacks might be expected. A part of the house which now stands at this point and is supposed to have been built by the French at this time, is now occupied by Mrs. Mary Barnes, the widow of the late Judge Barnes. This would make this dwelling the oldest one in existence along the lakeshore or possibly in the whole State of Vermont. The protection afforded by the forts resulted in the continued colonization of the lake shore by the French and during the next fifteen years, and settlements were extended some distance north of Chimney Point.

On the northern boundary of the Basin Harbor property near the shore of North Harbor, is an old burying-ground which contains about a dozen graves. One of these graves was opened up several years ago and a sword found in it, bearing a French inscription. The markers on the graves were just common field stone and it is the consensus of opinion that the persons buried there were those who passed away during the period of some twenty years that French settlers lived at Basin Harbor. During a thirty year period the French occupied Fort St. Frederic, a total of one hundred and ninety-eight deaths were recorded.

It was the dream of the early settlers to make this a New France, free from all of the turmoil and strife of the old country, and the people moved in on barges filled with their household goods, livestock, and many other things needed to conquer the wilderness. The records show that these

The French, Dutch, the English Strive

pioneers did considerable in the way of gardening, setting out fruits, such as apples, plums, currants, etc. The Fameuse apple was first introduced into Vermont at that time. However, all was not peace and quiet in the Champlain Valley.

It is difficult to picture the amount of traffic on the lake at the time of the French occupation. In 1736 there was a regular service of sailing vessels established between St. Johns and Fort St. Frederic. Many pieces of equipment, mill stones, cannon and ammunition were shipped over from France.

Peter Kalm, a Swedish traveler, made a trip down the lake in 1749 and wrote up a very good description of Fort St. Frederic which by that time had been developed into quite a formidable stronghold on which the French had expended a good many thousand livres. This is part of Kalm's description of the fort:

> "This fortress (Fort St. Frederic) is built upon a rock of black calcareous schist; its form is almost quadrangular; its walls, thick and high, are built of this same stone, of which there is a quarry about half a mile from the fort. A high and very strong tower, bomb-proof and supplied with cannons from top to bottom, defends the eastern part; there resides the governor. The enclosure of the fort has within it a pretty little church and stone houses for the officers and men."

Kalm informs us concerning the garrison and its life at the fort: "Each soldier receives a new coat every two years, and annually a waist-coat, a cap, a hat, a pair of breeches, a stock, two pair of socks, two pair of shoes, and wood as much as is needed in the winter. Their pay is five sous a day and amounts to thirty sous when they have some special duty to perform for the King's service . . . If a soldier falls ill, he is taken to the hospital where the King furnishes him a bed, nourishment, medicines, nurses and servants . . ."

Lake Champlain as the Centuries Pass

The ruins of this fort that remain show only an outline of its once strong walls.

There was a constant dispute between England and France as to who should control the lake and the surrounding valley. The French continued to send out raiding parties beyond their settlements and the colonial and English forces made many expeditions of retaliation.

While the French and Indian war had been going on for some time in other parts of America, its fury had not struck the Champlain Valley until 1755. The French had unquestioned possession of the lake for some twenty-four years and had made extensive settlements along both shores. These, however, were too close to the English settlements for comfort, hence plans were made in January 1755, to start a campaign which it was hoped would result in the capture of the French outpost at Crown Point. William Johnson of Mohawk, New York, who had achieved some fame in dealing with the Indians, was placed at the head of a large force of colonial troops and the Indian allies.

The French in Canada, learning of these plans, sent an army of several thousand men under the command of Baron Dieskau to go to the defense of Crown Point. Reaching Fort St. Frederic, in the early part of September, he did not stop there but led his troops forward to attack the colonial army between the lower part of Lake Champlain and Lake George. In the days that followed fierce battles were fought, and while at the start Dieskau had the best of the struggle, he was unable to organize his troops to follow up his advantage. In the end he was badly wounded and captured by General Johnson's forces. His troops retreated back to their boats on South Bay and to the shelter of Fort St. Frederic.

General Johnson made no attempt to follow up his victory and his army remained in camp at Lake George until the severe cold of the northern winter caused them to largely disperse.

The French, Dutch, the English Strive

Realizing the necessity of providing further protection for their settlements along the lake, the French decided to increase their fortifications on Lake Champlain. So in 1755, Marquis de Vaudreuil, Governor General of New France, sent Marquis de Lotbiniere down Lake Champlain from Montreal to see what place would be the most suitable for building an extensive and modern fort. After looking over Fort St. Frederic he went south to a present site of Fort Ticonderoga and started the layout of a fort of the type designed by the military expert, Vauban, of Europe.

Some two thousand men were reported to have been engaged in the task of building this fort. Larger ships were built at the northern end of the lake to convey the troops and supplies from the north and about this time the first French gun boat was equipped for use on the lake. It was during this period that the traffic on the lake was extremely heavy, both in summer with the boats coming up and down the lake, and in winter over the ice. All supplies, cannon, ammunition, and building equipment, must of necessity come down from the north. The walls of the fort were first made of logs with earth packed between them. However, during the summer of 1757 De Lotbiniere substituted stone for most of the logs he had used on the outer walls of the fort.

It was during the French and Indian War that Major Robert Rogers became famous and his exploits have been admirably described in Kenneth Roberts' "Rogers' Rangers." Major Rogers kept a journal of his daily doings, 1755-1760, which were published in 1883 and make interesting reading. In 1756, when hiding in the bushes on the lake shore, he writes - "nearly a hundred boats passed before them on the way to Ticonderoga." The next night, July 7, they rowed farther north towards Basin Harbor and attacked and captured a schooner anchored there. He adds, "Hid some casks of wine and brandy in very secure places. Anchored at Button Mold Bay." The small cove located

Lake Champlain as the Centuries Pass

about one half mile south of Split Rock, where Rogers was supposed to have hid the liquor is still known as Grog Harbor.

The British and colonial troops had established quite an elaborate fort at the south end of Lake George called Fort William Henry and General John Winslow in charge at that time, raised an army of colonial troops, built some sloops and whale boats on Lake George and planned to make an attack on Fort Ticonderoga. But this did not materialize. During the winter months both the garrisons at Fort William Henry and at Fort Ticonderoga were reduced to a large extent, due to the fact that there were not quarters suitable for housing any great number of men during the very cold winter weather.

It occurred to the French in Canada that the winter months might be an excellent time to make an attack on Fort William Henry, so in February 1757, the French sent a large war party down from Canada over the frozen surface of Lake Champlain. No expense was spared in fitting out this army which consisted of regulars, Canadians, and Indians. Records show that the cost of the expedition was about two hundred thousand dollars. The troops were well equipped with overcoats, blankets, bearskins to sleep on, tarpaulins to sleep under, spare moccasins, spare mittens, kettles, axes, needles, awls, flint and steel, and miscellaneous other articles were provided, all of which had to be dragged over the ice on the light Indian sledges. They also carried provisions along for twelve days journey. Arriving at Fort Ticonderoga they were joined by some of the troops there, and on March 19, 1757 made their way towards Fort William Henry with an army of sixteen hundred men. After marching three days along Lake George they neared the fort and prepared for a general assault. The British and Colonial troops, however, were able to ward off the attackers and after a poorly organized siege the French decided to return to Canada. The history books

The French, Dutch, the English Strive

relate that on their return trip up Lake Champlain, there was brilliant sunshine and that the troops marching over the surface on snowshoes were blinded by the insufferable glare of this bright sun on the snow and ice. Thus ended another unsuccessful attempt by the French to maintain control of the Champlain Valley.

The French, however, were not inclined to give up their strongholds on Lake Champlain without a very definite struggle. So in July 1757, General Montcalm came down the lake with another large force of troops made up of 7600 Frenchmen, Canadians and 1800 Indians. They arrived at Fort Ticonderoga and set up camp there. The fort had been greatly strengthened and it was thought that it could resist any and all attacks.

During the summer months preparations were made for another attack on Fort William Henry as the French considered that they must wipe out this fort in order to hold Lake Champlain. Montcalm made elaborate plans for attacking the fort, and carried along plenty of artillery to reduce the fort if it became necessary. However, on August 7 General Monroe, who was then in charge of the fort, raised a white flag and surrendered the stronghold to the French. The British army retreating to Fort Edward were attacked by the Indians with a very heavy slaughter although they had been promised safe passage. On August 15 Montcalm loaded the spoils into their boats and before departing, completely demolished Fort William Henry. The victorious army then returned to Ticonderoga and on August 29 Montcalm left for Montreal carrying news of his great victory. At that time it looked as though the French would be able to maintain their hold on the Champlain Valley.

By 1758, Fort Ticonderoga was nearly completed and was considered ready to resist any attacks which the British and Colonial forces might make. In July of 1758 General James Abercrombie gathered a large force at the head of Lake George

Lake Champlain as the Centuries Pass

and travelled down to the north end of the lake and made plans to attack what was then called Fort Carillon. The French forces under the command of Marquis de Montcalm were notified in time to prepare for the attack and were successful in throwing up a series of fortifications on the route leading towards the main fort. It was here that a fierce battle was fought on July 8, 1758, which resulted in the defeat of the British, with very heavy losses. The situation on Lake Champlain had reached quite a serious state, and it was obvious that if the British were to drive the French off the lake, special efforts and preparations would need to be made.

It was in July of the following year, 1759, that General Jeffrey Amherst, who succeeded General Abercrombie, advanced down Lake George to attack the fort. Amherst followed Abercrombie's route but instead of attacking, he proceeded to surround the fort. For some reason the French garrison had been greatly reduced. Montcalm had gone to the defense of Quebec, leaving General Bourlamaque in charge. He soon realized that the fort was not equipped and did not have sufficient supplies on hand to stand the siege, so after a few days Bourlamaque evacuated and left General Hebecourt with a small garrison to hold the fort. However, in spite of the heavy artillery fire which he maintained, the British advanced through the French lines and set up counter defenses. After three days of bombardment, Hebecourt decided that it was useless to attempt the defense of the fort further, hence he set fire to it and left a lighted fuse leading to the powder magazine. The fort was soon in flames and the magazine blew up with a tremendous explosion. Apparently the French had ample boats on hand to transport the entire French army to Isle au Noix, where he joined Bourlamaque.

So, on July 31, 1759, the French forces passed up the lake, taking with them all the artillery and supplies they could

The French, Dutch, the English Strive

transport. This was the last time the French flag was to be seen on ships passing down the lake.

Although the French had abandoned their settlements and forts along the lake, they continued to keep a fleet on the lake which cruised around north of Plattsburgh. During a storm, this fleet was sunk near the west side of the lake. The exact location where these boats went down had not been determined; however, they are supposed to have sunk with all of the armament on board. Mr. Paul Bilhuber has made some effort to locate the ships by use of a depth finder on his cruiser. These ancient relics will eventually be located and brought to the surface and will add more pages to the history of Lake Champlain.

The general location of the sunken ship is shown on a photomural in Basin Harbor Club lounge.

Soon after the French had abandoned the shores of the lake, the English started to fortify Crown Point, which had always been considered one of the most strategic spots on the lake. Lord Amherst was delegated to start the construction of a fort and a group of barracks. A very elaborate plan was developed and it was the general scheme to make this a permanent military fortification. The British Government spent about $10,000,000 on this establishment, which was a rather large sum for those days. The embankment thrown up around the fort completely hides it from view.

Despite the great preparation and huge expenditure, no battle was ever fought on this site and sad to relate, much of the stone work of this, and Fort St. Frederic, was despoiled and taken across the lake in winter on the ice and used to construct many of the stone dwellings now seen along the road leading to the Champlain bridge. Those who sojourn on the shores of Lake Champlain should make it a point to visit what remains of these old forts and, as they stand in the parade ground, try to visualize what took place there some two hundred years ago.

Lake Champlain as the Centuries Pass

Scarcely had the French left the shores of Lake Champlain when adventurous, English-speaking settlers began to come in, taking up in many cases, the clearings abandoned by the French settlers. Now began a contest of an entirely different type between the Governors of Albany and Governor Benning Wentworth of New Hampshire for the control of the eastern shores of Lake Champlain.

"A South View of the New Fortress at Crown Point...1759," by Thomas Davies. Courtesy, Winterthur Museum.

5

The Contest Continues for the Ownership of the Shores of Lake Champlain

BOTH GOVERNOR WENTWORTH of New Hampshire and Governors Colden and Tryon of New York attempted to make fortunes out of dealing in what was known as the "New Hampshire Grants," the name at that time for what is now the State of Vermont. While the New York governors issued grants for many thousand acres on our shore, those of Governor Wentworth, for much of the same property, were the ones which eventually prevailed. The title to all of our Basin Harbor property dates back to the Wentworth Charter issued in 1762. New York refused to recognize the validity of the Wentworth grants, so a bitter controversy continued which at times attained proportions of border warfare. Wentworth outdid the New York governors by sending Samuel Robinson of Bennington to plead the case of the New Hampshire grants before King George. The shrewd act of Governor Wentworth in granting certain lots of land to the Church of England and the Society for the Propagation of the Gospel proved to be an aid to Mr. Robinson, since he was able to secure the help of this society and the Church in pleading the case before the King. As a result, Robinson secured a decree from King George III in July 1767, to the effect that the Governor of New York should stop granting land until His Majesty could look into the matter. Governor Wentworth issued some one hundred thirty charters from which he had derived a handsome profit. The charters varied in price from $100.00 up to $700.00 and Governor Wentworth became extremely wealthy out of this real estate transaction. The Wentworth mansion in Portsmouth, New Hampshire, is a present-day example of the luxurious living of that era. With the beginning of the Revolutionary War, the strife for title to this area was temporarily ended and King George had nothing more to say about land titles.

It is doubtful whether the Church of England or the Society for the Propagation of the Gospel received any great return from Governor Wentworth's generous grant. However, having the church lined up on his side proved to be a great asset. It is interesting to note that the term "glebe" designating a certain plot has carried down to the present day. The land adjoining the original Basin Harbor property on the southeast is Glebe Lot #135. The owners pay no taxes on the land but in lieu of a tax a fixed fee. The present annual payment is $27.41 per year on 175 acres. Provision of land for a schoolhouse was very meager—one school lot for 25,000 acres.

One particular contest for the possession of land in this area took place at the falls in Vergennes. Colonel John Reid had been granted a tract of land four miles wide on both sides of Otter Creek from its mouth to Sunderland Falls by the Governor of New York. When Colonel Reid sailed up from the lake through the winding Otter Creek with a band of Scotch settlers, he found the New Haven Falls, now Vergennes, in the possession of settlers under the charter of the New Hampshire Grants. They had built houses and roads, erected a mill and had quite an extensive settlement there. Colonel Reid's doughty Scotsmen led by one Donald MacIntosh, dispossessed the New Hampshire men and took

The Contest Continues

"A View of the Falls of Otter Creek, Lake Champlain, North America," by Thomas Davies, 1766. Courtesy Royal Ontario Museum.

over the Falls. Word of this outrage eventually reached Ethan Allen, who soon arrived on the scene with a band of Green Mountain Boys. Colonel Reid and his men were packed off in boats for points south and were warned not to return again. This event is well described in Thompson's "Green Mountain Boys." The former owners took over and peace seemed restored in the settlement. However, it was not long before Colonel Reid was back again with a larger force, well equipped to defend themselves and this time the New Hampshire men were forced to retreat in the face of a superior band. Again Ethan Allen, accompanied by Seth Warner and Remember Baker and more than one hundred armed men came to the rescue of the settlers. They attacked Reid's establishment on August 11, 1773 and really gave the Scotsmen a hard time. An account of what happened has been handed down and shows the thoroughness with which Ethan Allen and his men dealt with the New Yorkers. On the day following this Otter Creek Episode, James Henderson wrote to a Mr. MacIntosh at Crown Point as follows:

Lake Champlain as the Centuries Pass

"Our Houses are all Burnt Down. The Grist Mill is All Put Down. The Mill Stones Brock and Throns in To The Crick, The Corn is all Destroed By There Horses, and When It Was Proposed That We Should Build Houses and Keep Possion, They Threatened to Bind some of us To a Tree and Skin us Alive. Therefore we think its imposable To us To Live hear in Peace."

Two important settlements on the lake previous to the Revolutionary War are noteworthy of mention. One is the foundation of Skenesborough, (Whitehall) in 1761 by Major Philip Skene who had taken an important part in the British army fighting the Indians and the French. He was the first one to explore the shores of the lake around Port Henry and established the first iron mines there. He can be considered one of the pioneers of the Champlain Valley having developed an extensive establishment at the south end of the lake where he had great hopes of maintaining an empire of his own.

In a similar manner William Gilliland came to the shores of the lake about 1765. The epic of his adventures would make a book in itself. It has been written up to some extent in the History of Westport under the title of "Bessboro." He had also been a soldier in the French and Indian War with the British army and received a grant of land for his services in the war. In addition, he bought the rights of several others and accumulated a total of 4,500 acres in one tract in the vicinity of Essex, New York and at the mouth of the Boquet River. Gilliland was responsible for naming a number of the towns in the area. The original name of Westport was Bessboro, Elizabethtown was named for one of his daughters. Willsboro was named for Gilliland himself. Other names which Gilliland brought over for Ireland were Janesboro, Charlottesboro and Milltown. He left a diary which relates much about the life on Lake Champlain at that time.

The Contest Continues

Both the Skene empire and Gilliland's vast holdings were confiscated during or after the Revolutionary War and Gilliland's dreams, particularly, came to a very sad ending.

Ethan Allen took a very active part in the strife between the two English colonial governments. The exertion of Ethan and his well-organized band of Green Mountain Boys was one of the determining factors in deciding which side would hold title to our shores. Thompson's "Green Mountain Boys," published in 1839, paints very vivid pictures of their exploits.

Ethan had quite a sense of humor. This side of his character has not been brought out to any extent. As an example, he liked to disguise his gang as Indians and throw a fright into New York State interlopers. The story of his handling of Dr. Sam Adams of Bennington is in all the Vermont history books. The doctor had talked big about how he would shoot Ethan Allen or anyone that molested his property. Ethan sent out a squad of "the boys" to fetch him in. The Colonel held a "trial"—the doctor was found guilty and was sentenced to be hoisted up beside the stuffed catamount of the Tavern sign. This caused great merriment and great humiliation to the proud Dr. Adams.

On another occasion, he personally captured two New York sheriffs, locked them in separate rooms on the same side of a farm house. During the night, he rigged up a straw man which he hung from a limb in sight of both windows. Then in the early dawn he waked one deputy at a time, telling him to look out the window and observe the fate of his companion. He then allowed him to escape; after the first man had hustled off at top speed, he waked the other; both escaped, thinking that the other had been hanged.

Legends of his owl calls and "Beech Seal" are well known.

After he had punished and humiliated the New York settlers enough, a price was placed on his head. He immediately drew up a poster offering a reward for two prominent

Lake Champlain as the Centuries Pass

New York officials. This reward poster had wide distribution through the Grants. For sheer nerve, bravado, and feats of strength, there is no equal in the Vermont records.

When in captivity in England, he is reported to have had a lot of fun at the expense of the English, always pointing out that he was one of the Green Mountain Boys. If he was a boy, the English wanted to know what the men were like. Ethan never lacked word to describe them.

On November 25, 1765, Joseph Allen, only son of Ethan, was born to his first wife, Mary. While he was in captivity in England in 1771, Joseph died. He wrote his brother, Herman:

> "But mortality has frustrated my fond hopes and with him, my name expires. My only son, the darling of my soul, who should have inherited my fortune and maintained the honor of the family."

There have been many Ethan Allens in Vermont since his day, many claimed to be descendants of the Vermont hero. There would appear, however, to be no direct descendants.

The visions of both Ethan and Ira Allen were far in advance of men of their era. Ira was the founder of the University of Vermont. Vergennes, Ethan felt, had a great future. The valuable water power provided for industry in a better manner than Burlington. There were transportation facilities through Otter Creek to Lake Champlain. The surrounding country had a variety of natural resources: iron in Monkton, timber for all sorts of building and manufacture, rich soil capable of producing big crops. In this respect, the land was far superior to either Connecticut or Massachusetts. Yes, Ethan Allen had visions of Vergennes becoming the leading city of Vermont, and named it in honor of Count de Vergennes, a famous French statesman. In the period following the French and Indian war, there was a rapid influx of English settlers who came to seek their fortunes in a new

THE CONTEST CONTINUES

and promising land. Here a home site could be secured for a small amount of cash and a few lucky settlers could pick up sites that had been improved by early French occupants.

6

Capture of Fort Ticonderoga

ON MAY 11, 1775, an event occurred which brought Lake Champlain to world-wide notice. Ethan Allen with a small band of Vermonters, known as the Green Mountain Boys, captured the great stronghold of Fort Ticonderoga, which had been considered almost impregnable. Having been improved following the evacuation of the French at the end of the French and Indian War, it was used to store military supplies. The winter following its capture, the cannon and ammunition were taken to Boston by General Knox and were subsequently used in the siege of Boston. Some forty-two strong sleds and eighty-one yoke of oxen were used to transport these heavy guns. The following day some of Ethan's band took possession of Fort St. Frederic at Crown Point. These daring feats caused considerable stir in the lakeshore community and many of these early settlers were members of the adventurous party. Major Samuel Beach, who was one of the several members of the Beach family of Connecticut who had recently settled in Vermont, is credited with having travelled on foot sixty miles in one day in order to notify the settlers to hasten to join Ethan Allen's forces. The date of his hike was only about three weeks after Paul Revere's famous ride.

Lake Champlain as the Centuries Pass

"Plan du Fort Carillon." Courtesy of Special Collections, University of Vermont Library.

Julia Dorr's poem, "The Armorer's Errand" aptly describes this feat:

> "He threaded the valley, he climbed the hills,
> He forded the rivers, he leaped the rills.
> While still to his call, like Minute Men
> Booted and spurred, from mount to glen
> The settlers rallied. But on he went
> Like an arrow shot from a bow, unspent,
> Down the long vale of the Otter, to where
> The might of the waterfall thundered in air."

There has been great argument between the Beach family descendants as to whether it was Gersham or his son Samuel who performed this remarkable feat. They were father and son, so what does it matter?

Following the capture of Ticonderoga, Benedict Arnold, who had aided Ethan Allen in the capture of the fort, secured a boat and went down the lake, capturing a British

The Capture of Fort Ticonderoga

sloop at St. Johns and destroying other shipping at this point. Congress was reluctant to continue the holding of these strategic points on the lake but both Allen and Arnold called their attention to the fact that if these outposts were abandoned about five hundred families northward toward Otter Creek would be left subject to attacks of the British and Indians. So it was finally decided to maintain the forts, also to fit out an expedition to attack the British forces on Canada. On August 30, 1775, after surmounting many difficulties, General Schuyler was ready to lead his force of twelve hundred men northward, and for the first time American soldiers traversed the broad lake highway past Basin Harbor. Settlers along the shore must have been greatly relieved to see this aggressive move which seemed to mean security for their homes.

After Montreal had been captured by the American troops, Congress sent a commission consisting of Benjamin Franklin, Samuel Chase and Charles Carrol to Canada to induce the Canadians to join forces with the colonists. The trip down the lake was made in any open scow boat thirty-seven feet long and eight feet wide. The party passed the night of April 24, 1776, with Peter Ferris at Arnold's Bay. Being on Lake Champlain in an open boat in April was a severe hardship for Benjamin Franklin, who was then seventy years old. He returned through the lake the last of May without having obtained the desired results.

With the failure to capture Quebec and the army being stricken with smallpox, a retreat was ordered and July 3, the retiring American troops sailed up the lake. A great many of the sick were cared for at Hospital Creek located just north of Chimney Point.

Undaunted, however, by their lack of success in Canada, the Colonial forces collected at Fort Ticonderoga and Benedict Arnold was appointed to take change of the fleet which was to be built at Whitehall and armed to resist the expected

Lake Champlain as the Centuries Pass

English invasion. It was well known that Carleton, the British Commander, was gathering a large force in Canada and building boats to convey troops, also warships to sweep the lake free from the enemy. Arnold's task of building and equipping a fleet was a most difficult one. Trees were cut and hauled to the mill, where they were sawn into boat timbers and planking. Some two hundred ship-carpenters were employed in building the boats. After the crafts were built and launched, there was the Herculean task of securing sails, guns, cordage, etc., all of which had to be hauled long distances. However, here was the beginning of the American Navy on Lake Champlain. By the last of August, 1776, Arnold had nine ships ready to sail. In his memoirs he says that he left Crown Point August 27 but encountering a strong wind, they anchored in Button Mould Bay until September 1. While anchored there the men on board came ashore for supplies and wood; perhaps they traveled over the land where summer visitors now drive golf balls! We can easily visualize this fleet sailing down "The Narrows" opposite Basin Harbor on a September day en route to Willsboro. They anchored there and Gilliland complained that Arnold's men did a lot of damage to his property. During the next few weeks several ships were sent to reinforce the fleet, which kept in continuous communication with the forts at the south. There was a total of sixteen ships in Arnold's fleet and he had assembled eight hundred men to man the vessels.

On Friday, October 11, 1776, the British and American fleets met in battle for the first time in history right here on Lake Champlain. Captain Mahan says, "It was a strife of pygmies for the prize of a continent." It was an uneven fight; as Trevelyan, the English historian, says, "Compared with Carleton's vessels, the American sloops and galleys were mere cockboats." Yet Arnold kept them busy from eleven o'clock in the morning until five in the afternoon. In spite of

The Capture of Fort Ticonderoga

the heavy damage done to the American fleet, Arnold says in his memoirs, "At sunset, the enemy actually retired, defeated."

Captain Pringle of the British fleet is said to have remarked, "We have winged the bird and will pick him up in the morning. He cannot escape us." However, Arnold had other plans; the night being dark and foggy, his ships were formed in line and cautiously made their way along the shore to the southward. A photo mural in Basin Harbor Club lounge shows the line of escape. He says," We went along the shore where they least expected us." Baron Riesdesel writes, "The astonishment of the British the next morning was great, as was Carleton's rage." The latter started off in pursuit in great haste and seeing an object in the fog, opened fire on what he supposed to be one of Arnold's ships. Upon examination, this proved to be a large rocky island, which to this day is called Carleton's Prize.

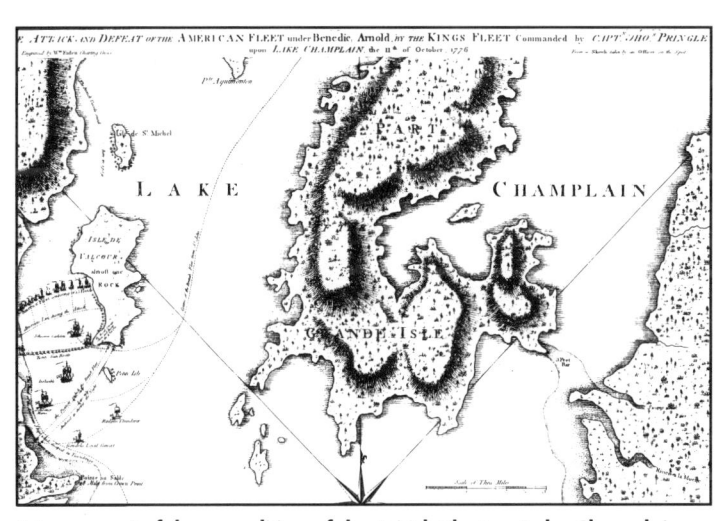

"An account of the expedition of the British Fleet on Lake Champlain, under the command of Capt. Thomas Pringle, and the defeat of the Rebel Fleet, commanded by Benedict Arnold, on the 11th & 13th of October, 1776." Printed for W. Faden, London.

49

Lake Champlain as the Centuries Pass

Arnold stopped at Schuyler's Island to make a few repairs on his badly shattered boats and the next day the retreat continued on against a south wind. By the time they had reached Split Rock, the British ships were alongside and a running battle was carried on for some two hours, as they passed through "The Narrows" opposite Basin Harbor. Settlers along the shore were terrified by the cannonading which echoed back from the Palisades and disturbed the Sunday stillness. They could easily see how the battle was going and many expected a British attack on their homes as soon as the fight should be over. Arnold, seeing that escape was impossible, ran his ships ashore in the harbor in front of Peter Ferris' house, where he set them afire, and with his force of men escaped over land to Crown Point. This spot has since been known as Arnold's Bay. The American Navy had been wiped out but, as Chadwick said, "Never had any force, big or small, lived to better purpose, or died more gloriously, for it had saved the lake for another year." A monument of the shore at Arnold's Bay commemorates this event.

In 1938 Paul Bilhuber secured a diving outfit and made an attempt to locate some of the cannon that Arnold threw overboard before beaching the boats. After a lot of travel over the muddy bottom, he came upon a cannon standing upright but well imbedded in the bottom. Its location was marked as it couldn't be moved. The next day our old scow boat was rigged up to use in raising the cannon. Lashed to the side of the scow, Mr. Bilhuber brought it to Basin Harbor. The following year he made a carriage for the cannon and it now guards the entrance of Basin Harbor, a constant reminder of the historic events which took place on our lake.

In October, 1951, L. F. Hagglund who had previously raised the "Philadelphia" and the "Royal Savage," two of Arnold's ships on the site of the battle, searched the bottom of Arnold's Bay, located what was left of one of the ships and raised it to the surface. Thus he has the remains of two of Arnold's fleet in his museum near Ausable Chasm.

The Capture of Fort Ticonderoga

"A Description of the Engagement on Lake Champlain." Printed for R. Sayer & J. Bennett, London. It illustrates the running battle on October 13, 1776, which passed Basin Harbor.

As soon as Arnold's fleet was out of the battle, the British advanced up the lake and occupied Crown Point, but finding that Ticonderoga was capable of resisting an attack, Carleton took his whole force back to Canada for the winter. This battle of Valcour Island was to the Navy what Bunker Hill was to the Army. A poorly-equipped force had demonstrated that it could ably oppose the best England could send against them. During the winter, the settlers along the shore were undisturbed by any invasion, although there

The cannon recovered from Arnold's Bay by Paul Bilhuber is now on exhibit at the Lake Champlain Maritime Museum.

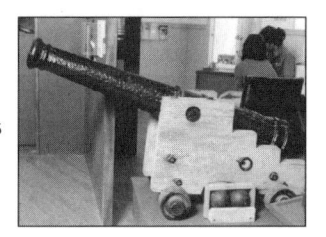

51

Lake Champlain as the Centuries Pass

was some apprehension that one might be attempted over the ice.

In the spring of 1777, scouts sent north reported a large force being made ready for an expedition up the lake. This British army, made up of about eight thousand troops, partly German Hessians and Indians, assembled at St. Johns June 12, 1777, and started southward, under the command of General Sir John Burgoyne. In addition to his military talents, General Burgoyne had the reputation of being quite a ladies' man and had written several successful musical comedies. The following is a verse from one of the songs:

> "Sing and Quaff
> Dance and laugh
> A fig for care and sorrow,
> Kiss and drink
> But never think
> 'Tis all the same tomorrow."

It required an amazing number of boats to convey so large a body of men. A young British officer, Captain Anburey, gives a striking picture of their passage down the lake. He says: "When we were in the widest part of the lake, whose beauty and extent I have already described, the whole army appeared in one view and in such perfect regularity as to form the most complete regatta you can possibly conceive."

Extracts from Field Diary of Lt. Thomas Anburey (Army of General Burgoyne), Published 1789 in London:

> . . . "We (four brigades) passed down the lake by brigades, seventeen to twenty miles a day. Second Brigade takes encampment of first and so on successively. . . Departure was always at daybreak. In front, Indians with birch canoes 20 or 30, then the advance corps in a line with the gunboats, then the Royal George and Inflexible

The Capture of Fort Ticonderoga

sloops and brigs, 1st Brigade of regulars then Generals Burgoyne, Reisdall and Dieskau, etc., then the 2nd Brigade followed by German Brigade, rear guard, sutlers and camp followers."

Letter 25 Camp at Boquet River...June 23, 1777: pp. 164..."Having proceeded thus far up the lake, I am enabled to give you some account of it, especially as we have passed the broadest part. There are many small islands dispersed in different parts and where it is widest, you are not able to discern the opposite shore. There are several plantations on each side, but they are more numerous on the south, the north side being lofty, rocky mountains. It abounds with great quantities and variety of fish, sturgeon, black bass and masquenouqez, pike of an incredible size and many others."

No trouble or expense had been spared by the British to provide Burgoyne with the best of everything for this expedition. It required many hours for this armada to pass Basin Harbor. It was the greatest force ever to be seen on Lake Champlain and made an astonishing military spectacle.

Here is Lt. Anburey's account of the encampment at Button Mold Bay:

> *Letter 26*
> Camp at Button Mold Bay
> upon Lake Champlain
> June 24, 1777.

My dear Friend:
Yesterday General Burgoyne had a conference with them (Chief Le Loup and his Indians). After the meeting of the Indians at River Boquet, the general ordered

them some liquor and they had a war dance...

This bay where our present encampment is, lies to the south side of the lake and derives its name from the pebbles of which great abundance are thrown up on the shores, the exact form of a buttonmold.

Just before we entered this bay there came a most violent and unexpected squall, occasioned by the land winds blowing from the top of the high mountains on the north side of the lake; it was but short duration, but terrible while it lasted. You will form some idea how powerful and with what violence it blows from these mountains from the following circumstances. A small brig, belonging to the fleet with very little sail was in an instant laid flat on her side and the crew was obliged to cut away to masts to make her rise again.

The lake was vastly agitated, you may easily judge how very dangerous it must have been to the small bateaux which are constructed with flat bottoms and quite ungovernable when it blows hard. Though the men who rowed the bateaux in which I was were continually relieved, it was with much difficulty they could bring her into this bay, their strength being almost exhausted. However, the whole brigade got safe, except two bateaux that were swamped just as they got close in shore but as it was not out of a man's depth, no lives were lost.

During this storm, I dreaded much the fate of Indians in their birch canoes . . . rose to every wave and floated like a cork.

A soldier got a fawn, presented it to his captain, put in on board the bateaux but during the storm it was washed overboard.

Tomorrow we embark from this place to Crown Point.

Yours,

The Capture of Fort Ticonderoga

On one of my travels recently, I encountered an Englishman who had just returned from Australia. In the course of conversation he mentioned reading an English book on the subject of sunken treasure on a world wide basis. This book stated that one of Burgoyne's ships carrying the soldiers' pay was sunk in Button Mold Bay during a storm. This presents another challenge to further exploration of the bottom of Lake Champlain.

Before Burgoyne's troops reached this section, the settlers along the shore had mostly abandoned their homes, withdrawing to safer places of abode, although the General had sent out proclamations in advance, stating that the settlers would be unharmed if they would support him, sell him their cattle and not enter into hostilities against his army; otherwise, he would send his Indians to kill and destroy. Prof. Crockett's *History of Lake Champlain* vividly depicts this flight: "Like hunted creatures before a prairie fire, the settlers poured out of the valley, hurrying southward through the pitiless forest, in mortal terror of the ever-present and awful danger of the scalping knife of the savage foe."

Extracts from the speech of General John Burgoyne to the Indian allies assembled on the Boquet River June 21, 1777, read as follows:

> "I Positively forbid bloodshed when you are not opposed in arms. Aged men, women and children and prisoners must be held sacred from the knife and hatchet even in the time of actual conflict. You shall receive compensation for the prisoners you take but you shall be called to account for scalps."

A photo mural depicting this event is on the walls of the Basin Harbor Club lounge.

The speech was little understood or heeded by his Indian cohorts who proceeded to scalp any settlers who were found

Lake Champlain as the Centuries Pass

along the shore of the lake. When reports came to Burgoyne of the slaughter of whole families, he was reported to have remarked, "It's a conquered country and we must wink at such things."

From *The Pioneer History of the Champlain Valley* by Winslow C. Watson, page 179 under date of June 16, 1776, is a quotation from an article written by R. G. Gleiger, a member of General Franzer's staff, a part of Burgoyne's army:

> "Here a scene of indescribable sublimity burst upon us. Before us lay the waters of Lake Champlain, a sheet of unruffled glass, stretching away some ninety miles to the south, widening and straightening as rocks and cliffs projected into the most fantastic shapes into its channels. On each side is a thick and uninhabited wilderness now rising up into the mountains, now falling into the glens while a noble background is presented towards the east by the Green Mountains whose summits appear even to pierce the clouds. On the west mountains still more gigantic in loftiness and pride and dignity. I cannot by any powers of the language do justice to such a scene."

On page 187 under the date of June 23, 1777, quoted from Hadden:

> "The fleet wrapt up in Otter Creek three miles on the western shore of the lake. This Creek is here about 100 yards wide and runs up the country more than 150 miles towards New England."

As Burgoyne's armada approached Fort Ticonderoga then in command of General St. Clair, there was nothing to prevent his landing troops wherever desired. They first captured Mount Hope which commanded a part of the American lines, and then cut St. Clair's communications with Lake George.

Soon one of General Burgoyne's engineers, Lieutenant

The Capture of Fort Ticonderoga

Twiss, decided that it was feasible to haul cannon up Sugar Hill as Mt. Defiance was then known. From this height the British could easily reduce the fort. General St. Clair decided that the fort must be abandoned, thus for the second time, this great stronghold fell without a shot being fired. The American force retreated across a foot bridge to Fort Independence on the east shore opposite Fort Ticonderoga, however, they soon abandoned that and were over taken by the British at Hubbardton where a fierce battle was fought. The result, however, was the loss to the British of the entire Champlain Valley.

Although Burgoyne's army met crushing defeat at Saratoga, British control of Lake Champlain still continued and there was no safety along these shores until the end of the Revolutionary War.

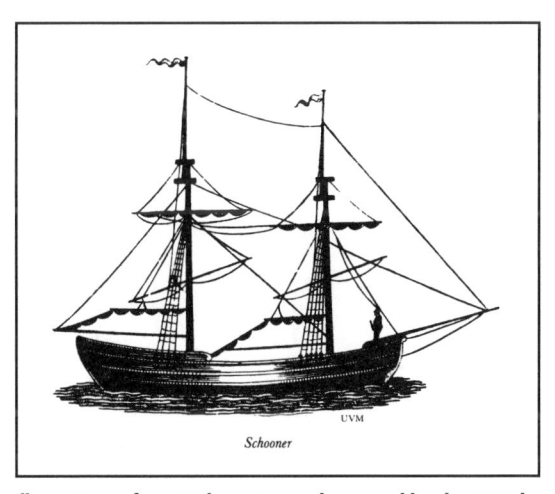

Illustration of an 18th century schooner, like the British schooner *Maria* on Lake Champlain. Courtesy of Special Collections, University of Vermont.

Lake Champlain as the Centuries Pass

During this period Captain Chambers, in charge of the British Fleet, sailing in the brig *Maria*, made a survey and map of the shores showing the depth of the water, etc. The maps were accompanied by detailed notes indicating where boats could anchor with safety and where they should guard against attack. The original maps and manuscript were recently secured in England by Mr. Howland, late President of National Life Insurance Company, and presented to the Vermont Historical Society. They are beautifully done by hand and are a valuable acquisition to the historical records of the Champlain Valley. On this chart Diamond Island appears as Sloop Island, Scotch Bonnet as Scotchman's Bonnet, Button Bay as Button Mold Bay, and Westport as Baye du Roches Fendu, meaning the Bay after Split Rock. The notes included the following instructions; "I would advise all people navigating on Lake Champlain to keep the west shore on board whilst they are below Split Rock during this

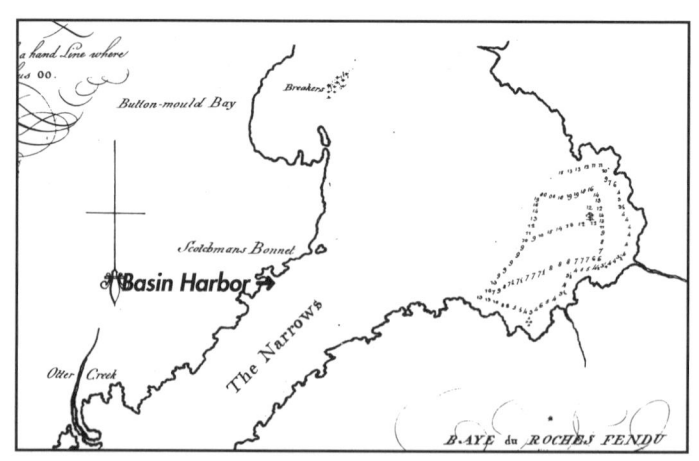

One of the maps from Captain William Chamber's ," Atlas of Lake Champlain," showing the part of the lake between Ferrisburg, Vermont and Westport, New York. From <u>Atlas of Lake Champlain 1779—1780</u>, printed by Vermont Heritage Press, Inc. and Vermont Historical Society.

58

The Capture of Fort Ticonderoga

war—if you should adventure too near the east shore, you may have some of your men picked off by the rebel scouts, as there is always a number of them out whenever the vessels are up the lake, in order to stop any friends of the government that may be coming into Canada, or to pick off any of the seamen should any officer venture to land a body of men from the vessel, which I would advise them never to do. Whenever wood is wanted there is plenty of islands on the western shore and there is no danger." (From this, it may be concluded that our shores were not entirely deserted.)

In 1778, several British raiding parties infested the shores, carrying off any settlers who remained, burning their homes and spreading destruction even more than Burgoyne had done. Some of the men captured were afterward returned from Canada; others died in captivity. Peter Ferris was one of the men seized during these raids.

In October, 1781, news of the surrender of Cornwallis reached the Champlain Valley and upon hearing of this, the British forces retreated into Canada.

In 1783 Washington and several of his officers visited Ticonderoga and Crown Point, but there is no evidence to show that he traveled farther up the lake. With peace restored to the Champlain Valley, the scattered inhabitants once more returned to rebuild their devastated homes and continue their struggle with the wilderness.

The Township of Ferrisburg

THE TOWNSHIP OF FERRISBURG is located on the shores of Lake Champlain and is typical of many areas up and down the shore. The charter of this township was granted on June 24th 1762 by Benning Wentworth to Benjamin Ferris and some sixty other subscribers. All land titles in this area are based on this charter.

In the original proprietors book of the Town of Ferrisburg, Timothy Rogers, Clerk records as follows:

> "At a legal meeting we had at Silas Gaige's in Ferrisburg in the month of May in the year 1785, which meeting was prescribed according to law, it was voted to give Silas Bingham the undivided rite to lot 6" Lot 6 was part of the present Basin Harbor Club property. Silas Bingham was the first recorded owner . . .
>
> ". . . and a spot was voted for a town site between Basin Harbor and Botin Mol Bay in said Ferrisburg."

Timothy Rogers was also a surveyor and with the assistance of David Brydia the area was laid out in house lots.

He goes on to tell about the laying out of the town site near the New Haven Falls which is the present City of

61

Lake Champlain as the Centuries Pass

Vergennes. I have an old map of the Basin Harbor-Button Bay area which shows a division into six lots extending from the lake shore to the west line of Glebe lot no. 135 there were apparently 40 to 50 acres in each lot.

On Oct. 2nd 1785, Timothy Rogers, still the Proprietor's Clerk has secured the town records from Benjamin Ferris who lived at Arnolds Bay. He was moving all of his household possessions by scow boat from the Button Bay area to Little Otter Creek Falls near Ferrisburg Center. The boat leaked so badly he unloaded the household goods on shore. During the night the campfire spread and his household goods along with the proprietor's records of the town of Ferrisburg were destroyed. This story has appeared in the History of Addison County and Hemingway's Gazetteer. It was generally thought that the Charter was burned with the other town records. In December, 1951, while searching through old town records, I came on the original record of the fire in Timothy Rogers' handwriting. Here is the explanation Rogers gave of having his "ritings bornt" as it appears in Book 1 of Ferrisburg Town Records:

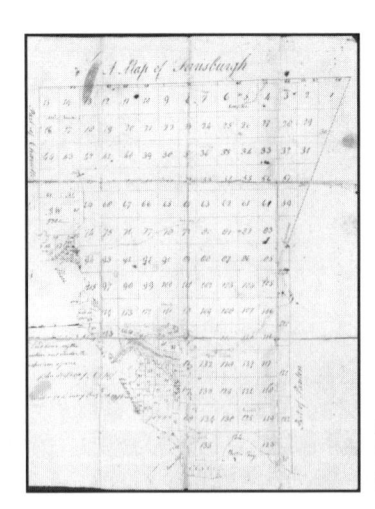

A copy of the original town lots located in the Town of Ferrisburg's Town Clerks' office.

The Townshiip of Ferrisburg

On the sekont day of the 10 month about mid nite or a litle after I landed below letill orter forls by the sid of the bay for I had ben moving from botin bay in ferrisburgh to letill orter crik forls. i had bote the farm of Wilam Ward. we landid the best of our goods on the bank for i was afrad the bote would sink. it was a dark rany time and my wife was sik. after we got some fir we went through the woods about a quarter of a mild to a hous. My men cindild a fir by the side of a tree by which we had campt which bornt down before morning and fel rite acrost my goods that was landid and bornt almost all my valabill housill goods. A large chist of droys was bornt with all my notes, bonds deads with the proprietors records of this town ferrisburgh-for I was proprietors clerk and had got the records from Benjamin Ferris who had cept the records before the late war. He had the records and charter. I got the records and not the charter.

From this it seems likely that the charter must be in existence somewhere. Mrs. Elizabeth Robinson, who has been Assistant Town Clerk for the past forty odd years said she had never seen the charter in any of the town records, but with this statement of Rogers that he did not have the charter when the records burned, Mrs. Robinson began a thorough search through the drawers and pigeon holes of the old town safe. In the bottom of a drawer under other papers was a small envelope, yellowed with age, which contained the original Benning Wentworth charter! The 190-year-old parchment document had been folded so many times that it was about to fall apart. It was difficult to assemble the parts for photostatting, but a great satisfaction to have been of assistance in getting this old document brought to light and to have copies made for the use of future generations. The area granted in these charters was about six square miles and contained approximately 25,000 acres. There were usually sixty-four proprietors' rights, each to have upwards of 360 acres of land. One of these "rights" was reserved as a "glebe" for the Church of England and one for the first settled minister, one for a school and one for the Society for the Propagation of the Gospel in Foreign Parts and two for the Governor himself. Governor Wentworth, the sly old bird, apparently had his surveyors pick out the choice sites for his land and where possible, he had his lots adjoin those of other townships so in some cases, he had some two thousand acres in one plot.

Here is how the Ferrisburg Charter starts:

Province of New Hampshire.
G E O R G E the Third,
By the Grace of God, of Great Britain, France and Ireland,
KING, Defender of the Faith, &c.
To all Persons to whom these Present shall come,
Greeting.

A photostat of both sides of the charter listing the names of the proprietors and the map of the division of the lots can be seen in the Basin Harbor museum.

Platt Rogers was one of the early permanent settlers on the shores of Lake Champlain.

He was a man of many talents—a surveyor, road builder, mine operator and shipbuilder. Born December 30, 1739, at Fishkill, New York, he was named for a member of the Platt family, who later on settled in Plattsburgh, New York. At the age of twenty-five, he took Eyda (Dutch for Ida) Wiltsie for his bride. They were married on April 2, 1764. About twelve years later, he joined the army and took a prominent part in the Revolutionary War, coming out with the rank of Captain. Following the War, he was engaged in road building and surveying for the State of New York. In 1789 he was

The Township of Ferrisburg

laying out the road through the Schroon Lake area to Plattsburgh, New York. This was known for years as the old Rogers' road. I was able to secure the map of this road from the Historical Society in Albany. For this laborious work he received a road patent to some 16,000 acres of land in the Adirondacks area. It is quite interesting to note that with all of this land at his disposal, he decided to come over to Vermont, paying a comparatively high price for the Basin Harbor property.

Rogers kept a field book which is now in the library of Elizabethtown, New York. Under the date of July 15, 1789, he notes: "Had our batto hall-d acrost and went up Lake George about eight miles." Under the date of July 20, 1789 he notes, "the majority of the land (this was on the way to Schroon) is mountainous, hilly, rocky and rough, although some good valleys and small interval, a large quantity of very fine maple, also all kinds of timber that is common in this country."

He spent the latter part of the next summer exploring the Vermont shore of Lake Champlain, using a batteau which was brought over from Lake George. He stayed around the lake quite late and on November 11, 1790 made his first land purchase in Vermont.

Silas Bingham, who appears to have been the first person of record to own the Basin Harbor property, didn't own his original "rite" long for on page 1 of Book 2 of the Ferrisburg Town Records is a copy of the deed dated November 11, 1790 from David Callender to Platt Rogers. Callender states that he purchased the land from Silas Bingham. The deed calls for one acre "on the north shore of Bason Harbor" and the consideration was ten pounds. As this was a pretty high price for one acre of ground, there must have been some improvements on the property. At this time Rogers was fifty-one years of age, had a family of four daughters and four sons. One daughter, Mary, then twenty-one, had married Jared Pond.

Lake Champlain as the Centuries Pass

This was still pretty much pioneer country when Rogers made his first purchase here, as only a couple of years before this a British warship was patrolling the lake, making a depth chart and survey. Ethan Allen, the famous hero of Vermont, had passed away during the previous winter. Vermont had not as yet been admitted to the United States, being an independent republic at that time. So when Rogers moved up from Fishkill, New York to his new home on the shores of Lake Champlain, the matter of transportation presented quite a problem. While no records indicate the route or the mode of travel, it seems certain that the trip was made mostly by boat, first up the Hudson and then over the old military road built by Burgoyne to Lake Champlain. There Rogers is supposed to have had his own sail ferry boat. It required several trips to Whitehall to get everything transported to Basin Harbor. There were oxen, carts, various tools, crates of poultry, household furniture, various and sundry equipment. He also brought some slaves with him. The Dutchess Country records show that he owned six slaves. The only ones mentioned are Primas and Parmelia Storms, who lived with him for many years and were finally given their freedom and a plot of ground about a mile from Basin Harbor. They are both buried in the old Basin Harbor cemetery. Primas lived to be one hundred and seven years old.

On June 9, 1791, Rogers made his second purchase of land in the Basin Harbor area. The deed was signed by David Brydia and the land is described as follow: "Bounded on the east by Lot #138, on the south by the Glebe lot and on the west by Lake Champlain and a lot of land voted to Silas Bingham on the original rites of John Burling, this tract including Bason Harbour, is pitched and surveyed on the original rites of Vollentine Perry, Josiah Akins, Samuel Barr, Isaac Winn, Walter Franklin, James Nevins, being the full and undivided land of their said rites."

The Township of Ferrisburg

This was apparently quite a big plot of ground and the consideration was 116 pounds and 10 shillings of lawful money. This original deed and photostats of several others have been preserved in our historical collection at Basin Harbor.

Rogers had continued to purchase land during the time that he lived at Basin Harbor so before he died in Plattsburgh on October 7, 1798, he had acquired much of the land on the west side of Otter Creek, a total of over 2,000 acres. For this he had expended around $1,647.00 and for other purchases English money was used in the amount of 669 pounds and some shillings. The amount Rogers paid per acre varied a great deal. The average was about $3.50 an acre. In one case, Peter Field deeded him 33 acres for one Spanish dollar. Some of the deeds indicate that there were improvements on the land such as "together with all singular rights, members, improvements, purtenances to the same belonging or in any way pertaining thereto."

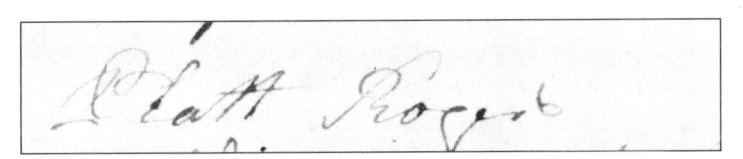

The signature of Platt Rogers, courtesy of the Ferrisburg Town Clerks' office.

"On April 16, 1798, the proprietors of the undivided lands of the town of Ferrisburg met at the house of Zebulon Crittenden and voted Platt Rogers moderator to govern said meeting." After Rogers passed away on October 7, 1798, at the next meeting of the proprietors at Crittenden's house they "voted to appoint Ananias Rogers, son of Platt and John Bishop, surveyors, to complete the ascertainment of the said proprietors' undivided land in lieu of Platt Rogers, deceased." He had apparently been making a survey of the town's undivided land. Ananias Rogers was listed as agent for the heirs of the late Platt Rogers and then Ananias and Jacob Rogers were voted administrators.

The Rogers' estate called for a lot of surveying and John Bishop had many assistants and presented an itemized expense account totalling 152 pounds, 18 shillings and 8 pence. Ananias Rogers received 1 shilling and 25 pence per day for 25 days for surveying and calculating the land. They boarded around while doing the job and in one case paid 2 pounds, 66 shillings and 6 pence for sixteen days' board. They started off with two quarts of gin, which cost 75 shillings and 75 pence. On the eighth day another quart of gin cost 37 shillings and 5 pence. It would seem that gin wasn't very cheap in those days but they made a quart last a while! In 1954 we paid $100.00 per day for a surveying crew but no gin was provided.

With the passing of Platt Rogers, the little empire that he had acquired was gradually sold off; only the old Homestead and the Lodge property were kept in the family. He had agreed to set his slaves free after a certain period of service but apparently did not do so before he died. However, the family, knowing his wishes, sold them a plot of ground from the Rogers' estate November 4, 1802 for a consideration of $120.00. Thus, on that date, Primas and Parmelia Storms not only became free citizens but landholders as well. This may have been the first deed on record where Vermont land was conveyed to a negro slave. Ten people signed the deed: Ida, Thomas, Ananias, Jacob, Syche, Platt, Jr., John and Phebe Halstead, Jared and Mary Pond. They built a cabin on the property and set out an apple orchard. The land was located on the road from Basin Harbor to Kellogg's Bay at the right angle left turn toward Kellogg's Bay. In my boyhood days, it was still known as the "negro orchard".

While Platt and Eyda Wiltsie Rogers were the parents of

The Township of Ferrisburg

eight children, none of them were born at Basin Harbor. The four sons, Thomas, Ananias, Jacob and Platt, Jr. were not known to have married. Of the daughters, Mary, born in 1769, died 1854, had married Jared Pond and inherited the land where the Lodge now stands. They were both buried on the knoll near the 18th green. Phebe, born in 1771, died 1816, married John Halstead and lived in Westport, New York. Ida, born in 1781, died in 1853, married James Vinans who later on inherited the Basin Harbor property. Syche never married.

It is possible to read between the lines in the old records and family agreements that some of the Roger's children were slightly deficient in many respects. Photostats of a number of these agreements are in the Basin Harbor museum. Thomas, Jacob, Syche and Platt, Jr. were labeled "queer" and not like other people. Ananias, however was named after his grandfather Rogers, was a man of ability and carried on his father's business, did surveying, held town offices and his name is found on many of the old deeds.

While Jacob Rogers may have been "off the beam" at times, he did negotiate one deal that really stands out. He evidently acquired title to some land north of Basin Harbor from his father's estate. By 1808 the population had increased to a point were it seemed necessary to provide a place of education for the children of the community. The original charter didn't provide a school site in this part of the town. A board of Trustees was formed consisting of Jared Pond, Stephen Beach and John Shull. They entered into an agreement with Jacob Rogers whereby he was to "lease and rent and convey to the said trustees as long as grass grows and water runs, the whole of the land on which a new house is now built in Ferrisburg near the dwelling house now occupied by John Brown, together with said house and the privileges and purtenances thereto, paying thereof yearly and every year on the first day of January forever hereafter to the said Jacob Rogers and his heirs and assigns, five cents, if demanded, yearly, provided always that these presents are upon this express condition that if the said leased premises shall at any time hereafter be occupied or used as a dwelling house, storehouse or the like for the space of six days, then in such case, that at any time thereafter it shall and may be lawful for the said Jacob Rogers, his heirs and assigns, in the said leased premises to enter the same and have it again as his former estate; and the said Jared Pond, Stephen Beach and John Shull, for themselves and their successors, hereby authorize and empower the said Jacob Rogers, his heirs and assigns, to put out and move and expel from the said premises all and every person or persons, thing or things that might thus be therein, anything herein or any lawful customary usage to the contrary notwithstanding."

The schoolhouse referred to is the old stone structure on the road to Kellogg's Bay known as the Basin Harbor district School No. 10. The very large natural face stone in the structure came from the farm of my great-grandfather, Stephen Beach.

In 1956, this old stone schoolhouse was advertised for sale to the highest bidder by the Ferrisburg school board. Since it was generally recognized that the Beach family could claim the building because of the reverter clause made by Rogers, no bids were submitted.

For a small sum the town officials gave us a quit claim deed to this old building. Now the question is how to get it moved to Basin Harbor.

8

The War of 1812

AFTER A COMPARATIVELY short period of peace, it was evident that war parties were again to enter the Champlain Valley. In 1809 Lt. Melancthon Taylor Woolsey was sent by the U. S. Navy to build two gunboats for the defense of the lake. In her "Bessboro," Mrs. Royce tells us that these ships were built at the well-established boatyard at Basin Harbor. We know that part of the machinery in this shipyard belonged to the Government from the report of the Commissary of Military Stores of 1804, which mentions "one pair iron gin blocks, brass sheaves, found at Basin Harbor in possession of Mr. Rogers." Then the next year's report mentions "two Iron Jack screws in possession of the assignees of Platt Rogers" on Lake Champlain.

In March, 1810, Lt. Sidney Smith was made commander of the operation on Lake Champlain and made his headquarters at Basin Harbor. The Growler and The Eagle, each carrying eleven guns, also four other gunboats, had been built there.

Crockett in his "History of Lake Champlain" stated that at the beginning of the War of 1812, the entire navy on Lake Champlain, consisting of two ships in bad repair, was stationed at Basin Harbor. On September 12, 1812, Lt. Thomas

Lake Champlain as the Centuries Pass

Macdonough was appointed by President Madison to take command of the naval forces on Lake Champlain. He came over from Portland, Maine on horseback through a notch in the White Mountains, the trip requiring four days. At that time, he was twenty-nine years of age, having been in the Navy since he was seventeen. He had distinguished himself in the war against the pirates of Tripoli in the Mediterranean and was considered one of the leading naval men of the era.

On June 3, 1813, Macdonough sent two sloops, the Growler and The Eagle, under the command of Lt. Sidney Smith to attack the British boats that were cruising around the northern part of the lake. On the approach of the American Ships, the British retreated into the Richelieu River, sailing up towards Fort Isle au Noix (Isle of Nuts). Lt. Smith was quick to pursue them. However, this proved to be a mistake on his part for after he got up the Richelieu River, he found that he could not maneuver the clumsy craft very well and both the sloops and the men on board were captured by the British. There was a well-established shipyard at Isle au Noix, now a Canadian museum called Fort Lennox, and the British re-equipped these American boats and named them The Finch and The Chub. For the rest of the summer and the next year, they were used by the British against the Americans to the great dismay of the latter. Macdonough continued to make his headquarters in the Inn at Basin Harbor, then owned by the James Winans' family. It was pretty obvious that the shipyard at Basin Harbor was too vulnerable to attack by the British and Macdonough began to look around for a more favorable site for building the much needed fleet. He finally selected Vergennes, eight miles from the mouth of Otter Creek as a suitable place to build the ships. These were going to be needed in a hurry to repulse the British fleet which was being built at Isle au Noix and St. Johns. This location was not an easy one for the British to reach as Dead Creek prevented an attack from the west and troops in

The War of 1812

Burlington guarded the northern approach. There was an abundance of timber adapted to shipbuilding and at that time Vergennes had several industries, including a blast furnace, iron foundry, forges, rolling mill, wire factory, grist mills and saw mills. All these were considered an aid to the work at hand. In the spring of 1814, Vergennes was the scene of great activity; hundreds of shipbuilders had been sent up from the coast and a large force was employed in cutting and hauling logs to the mills, where they were sawed into ship material. The first boat was launched in forty days from the time the trees were cut down. We can picture something of the hustling scenes enacted at the foot of the falls that spring. There were probably more people in Vergennes that at any former time or at any since.

With a British fleet cruising about the lake, there was some fear that boats might be sunk in the channel at the mouth of Otter Creek, thus bottling up Macdonough's fleet. This caused a force of men to be sent to fortify the point at the north of the river. Earthworks were thrown up and cannon mounted under the direction of Lt. Cassin, and both the fort and the point have since borne his name. As a further precaution, a dugout or canal was cut through the narrow strip of land separating Otter Creek from Kellogg's Bay so that his ships could reach the lake should the British be successful in blockading the mouth of the river. The entrance to this canal, called The Dugway, may still be seen, and the writer has passed through it in a boat during high water periods.

There was great excitement in the country 'round about when, early on Saturday morning, May 14, 1814, the British fleet appeared on the scene and opened fire on Ft. Cassin. The fire was returned by the battery and after an engagement of an hour and a half, resulting in some damage to both sides, the fleet drew off to the north. Many local people were engaged in this battle; the Field family, then living at

Lake Champlain as the Centuries Pass

Kellogg's Bay, alarmed by the attack, moved over to the farm then occupied by the writer's grandfather (and namesake) Allen P. Beach. The story is that the Field's family silver was buried in the garden before they left their lake shore home. This battle does not seem like a very serious affair now but with the Palisades echoing the roar of the cannon, and with loved ones actually taking part in the combat, it doubtless was an occasion for great anxiety.

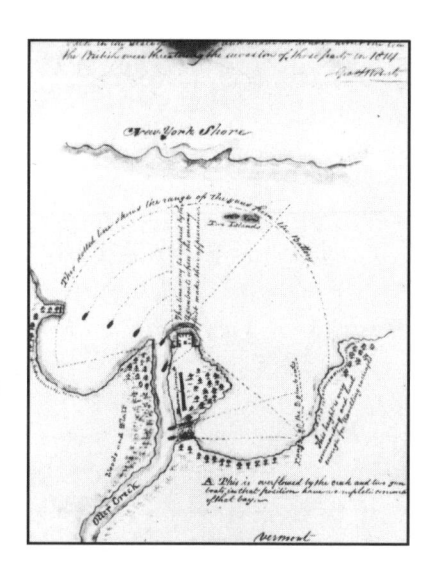

A contemporary map showing the defense at the mouth of Otter Creek. That land battery has come to be known as "Fort Cassin." Courtesy of the New York State Archives.

On May 26, Macdonough came down Otter Creek with nine of his boats and others were to follow at a later date. Throughout the summer, the fleet patrolled the lake and there was no engagement with the enemy until September. On Sunday morning, September 11, the British fleet was observed in progress up the lake off Cumberland Head. With great care, Macdonough arranged his ships in an advantageous position in Plattsburgh Bay, so that the enemy in approaching had to come up against the wind, making it difficult to maneuver their craft.

The War of 1812

Macdonough's boats were at anchor but the cables were so arranged that they could be transferred from one end of the boat to the other. This enabled him to turn his ships and discharge one broadside at the enemy while loading the other. The battle resulted in a complete victory for the American Navy and Captain Downie, the British commander, was killed in the engagement. Some of the British boats were sunk, others were captured and a few small boats escaped into Canada. This has gone down in history as one of the decisive battles of the war and was the last to be fought on Lake Champlain. While this naval battle was in progress, American forces were engaged with the strong British army on land near Plattsburgh. Seeing the defeat of the fleet and being strongly repulsed on shore, the entire British land forces withdrew into Canada. The captured ships were taken up Lake Champlain to Whitehall, dismasted and stripped of

"McDonough's Victory on Lake Champlain," 1816. Engraving published by B. Tanner, Philadelphia. Courtesy of Jane Maloney.

Lake Champlain as the Centuries Pass

cannon. A traveler passing through the lake in 1819 mentions seeing the ships there.

"A curious incident occurred on his (Commodore Macdonough's) ship "Saratoga" during the engagement. The hencoop was shot away and a rooster, thus released, flew into the rigging and flapping his wings, crowed out a lusty defiance to the enemy's guns. There he remained, flapping his wings and crowing until the engagement was over. The seamen regarded the event as encouraging and fought like tigers while the cock cheered them on."

Two photo murals depicting this battle adorn the walls of the lobby of the Basin Harbor Club.

Among the many local residents who took part in the battle of Plattsburgh was Captain Jared Pond, then living where The Lodge now stands. A letter has been handed down which Mary Pond, his wife, wrote on the day of the battle; she mentions hearing the cannonading distinctly at Basin Harbor and that it sounded much nearer than Plattsburgh. She states that on Monday night the house and barns were filled with soldiers from the south, evidently reinforcements on their way to Plattsburgh.

With the return of peace, life in the Champlain Valley resumed its former activities. Many of the soldiers who had visited this section during the war returned to make permanent homes there.

9

Ferry and Steamboat Service on Lake Champlain

IT ISN'T KNOWN WHEN the first ferries operated across Lake Champlain. The problem of getting across lakes and rivers with any sort of equipment is an ever-present one in any pioneer country. Obviously, there was no regular ferry service as long as there were war parties passing up and down the lake.

The first mention I have found of this form of transportation is related in William Gilliland's diary when on July 10, 1765, he mentions having "some New England men ferry his cattle across from a point he calls Cloven Foot to Cloven Rock, a former name for Split Rock." The cattle had been driven up from Albany to Crown Point, where four men succeeded in making them swim across the lake at Chimney Point. Apparently there was no ferry there at that date. The cattle were driven along the shore through the woods to "Cloven Foot." Looking at the outline of the shore, the only place where the undulations look anything like a foot is at Kingsland Bay, which would have been a logical place for a ferry.

When Platt Rogers started to take an interest in Vermont real estate in 1789, he realized the need of ferry service and established some sort of intermittent service from Basin

Lake Champlain as the Centuries Pass

"Sail Ferry from Arnold's Bay Panton to Westport, New York: In the 1880's, owned by Pat Sinon." Courtesy of the Lake Champlain Maritime Museum.

Harbor to Rock Harbor, which is south of Split Rock and provided a more protected landing place. At a later date a ferry was operated by Roger Alden Hiern who lived in Willsboro but owned land at Kingsland Bay and built a road across the "slang" to the stone house now owned by Ecole Champlain called Heirn's Ferry Road. General Samuel Strong was interested in this turnpike.

The ferry itself was known as the Grog Harbor Ferry. This ferry was most certainly propelled by sail and in order to tack back and forth called for quite a bit of seamanship. The boat was doubtless the batteau or scow type, possibly with lee boards on the sides.

Ferries operated across rivers at this period were usually propelled by poles and by ropes extending across the river and run through guides at the side of the ferry. One of these was operated by Zebulon Crittenden at a bend of Otter Creek about two miles up the stream. Another was located at a point where Basin Harbor road meets Otter Creek. This was operated by the Gaige family. An old account book of John Halstead lists a ferry payment of 12 1/2 cents to Gaige.

Ferry and Steamboat Service

As late as 1895, one of this type ferries was still operating across Otter Creek by Joseph Larrow. A steel cable running through pulleys had replaced the rope. The procedure, after pushing the scow-type ferry away from the shore, was to grasp the cable at the forward end of the ferry and walk towards the stern pulling on the cable. Two persons could in time get the ferry to the opposite shore. On one of these trips when in my early teens, I wanted to help, against the advice of the operator; the ferry had quite a bit of momentum when I gave a hand and came near losing a finger as I didn't let go of the cable quick enough, catching a finger between the steel cable and the pulley.

After about 1800, ferrying came to be important business on Lake Champlain with competition entering the field. Soon laws were passed by the Vermont Legislature granting ferry rights for specified periods of time. Certain requirements had to be complied with as to the regularity of the service and the load the ferry would carry. Even with the coming of the steamboat in 1809, ferry boats continued to thrive. One of the most important crossing places was from Arnold's Bay, then called Ferris Bay, to Barber's Point, a distance of about two miles.

With ox teams, wagon, flocks of sheep and cattle to transport, it was important to have as much open deck space as possible so the mast was placed on the side of the boat. That made it possible to drive through the center of the boat. Maneuvering a boat with this sort of a rig called for a lot of dexterity. This type of ferry was still in operation about 1900. The writer had a thrill riding on this quaint ferry some sixty years ago.

The first steamboat on Lake Champlain and second in the world to operate on a regular schedule was built by John and James Winans.

The Winans family, who resided at Basin Harbor for nearly one hundred years, was of Dutch origin, the same as

Lake Champlain as the Centuries Pass

Platt Rogers; thus, while the Dutch government didn't succeed in getting a permanent foothold in the Champlain Valley, many of that nationality eventually settled in this area, including Charles Platt who founded Plattsburgh.

John Winans was born in Dutchess County in 1766 and James in 1768. Some thirty years later they had a well-established shipyard at Poughkeepsie, New York. Along in 1806, Robert Fulton had a plan for building a steam-propelled boat to navigate the Hudson. He was able to get Chancellor Livingston, one of the wealthy land owners living on the Hudson to finance the construction. Livingston agreed to do the financing with the understanding that his friends, James and John Winans, were to build the hull of the ship. This was completed in 1807, the ship was taken to Brown's shipyard in the East River and there fitted out with engine, boiler, side wheels, et cetera. This information, in some ways contrary to the writings of others, was secured from old Winans' family records. The boat was named the *Clermont*, this being the name of the Livingston estate on the Hudson.

Detail showing what is believed to be the only surviving illustration of the lake's first steamboat, the *Vermont*. From a circa 1810 watercolor of "Bason Harbour, Lake Champlain," by Archibald Robertson.

Ferry and Steamboat Service

It is not known at just what date the Winans' brothers came to Basin Harbor. Doubtless they had visited Basin Harbor before Platt Rogers died in 1798. However, they had a thriving shipyard at Poughkeepsie and it was not until after the *Clermont* was completed that they began to get ideas about the possibilities of steamboating on Lake Champlain.

In 1808 they were able to organize a company in Burlington to finance a shipyard and the construction of the steamer which they christened *Vermont* when it was launched in 1809. This boat was larger than the *Clermont*, being one hundred and twenty feet long with twenty foot beam and draft of eight feet. The cost was $20,000.00, a sizable amount at that time. It was equipped with a twenty horsepower steam engine and had a top speed of eight miles per hour.

By 1809 the Winans were living at Basin Harbor and it was from here that the second steamboat in the world began to operate on a regular schedule. James had married Ida Rogers, daughter of Platt, and this was their home from then on.

The steamboat operation was interrupted by the War of 1812 but was resumed after the war. This steamer finally sank in the Richelieu River in 1815. The engine and other parts were removed and used in another boat. The hearth of the Homestead dining-room fireplace has an iron plate that came out of the old Winans steamer. In 1953, the old hull was raised by Captain Hagglund and is to become a part of a marine museum near Ausable Chasm.

In the 1820's an important new type of ferry came into use. It was invented by Mr. B. Langdon of Whitehall, New York. No longer was the modern ferry boatman dependent on the fickle wind, as this new ferry was propelled by a horse-power through paddle wheels on the side. Here is the way a traveler on the lake in 1820 describes the ferry:

81

Lake Champlain as the Centuries Pass

"The ferry-boat is of most singular construction. A platform covers a wide, flat boat. Underneath the platform, there is a large horizontal solid wheel, which extends to the sides of the boat; and there the platform, or deck, is cut through, and removed, so as to afford sufficient room, for two horses to stand on the flat surface of the wheel, one horse on each side, and parallel to the gunwale of the boat. The horses are harnessed, in the usual manner for teams—the whiffle trees being attached to stout iron bars, fixed horizontally at a proper height into posts, which are a part of the fixed portion of the boat. The horses look in opposite directions, one to the bow and the other to the stern; their feet take hold of channels, or grooves, cut in the wheels, in the direction of radii; they press forward, and, although they advance not, any more than a squirrel in a revolving cage, or than a spit dog at his work, their feet cause the horizontal wheel to revolve, in a direction opposite to that of their apparent motion; this, by a connection of cogs, moves two vertical wheels, one on each wing of the boat, and these, being constructed like the paddle wheels of steamboats, produce the same effect, and propel the boat forward. The horses are covered by a roof, furnished with curtains, to protect them in bad weather; and do not appear to labour harder than common draft horses, with a heavy load.

The inventor of this boat is Mr. Langdon, of Whitehall, and it claims the important advantage of simplicity, cheapness and effect. At first view, the labour appears like a hardship upon the horse, but probably this is an illusion, as it seems very immaterial to their comfort, whether they advance with their load, or cause the basis, on which they labour, to recede."

Ferry and Steamboat Service

In 1950 when en route to Florida, I stopped over in Washington and took a look at the U. S. Patent Office on the bare chance that Langdon had taken out a patent on his invention. Somewhat to my surprise, I had placed in my hands the plans which were submitted by Mr. Langdon when his idea was patented on June 5, 1819. At a later date, I secured copies of these plans.

On October 21, 1821, the Vermont Legislature granted a charter to H. H. Ross and Charles McNeill to operate a horse ferry between Charlotte, Vermont and Essex, New York. This ferry used six horses, three on each side and was in operation until 1827 and proved to be a very popular route across Lake Champlain. A newspaper of the era carried an advertisement describing the service offered between Westport and Basin Harbor on the Horse-Boat *Eagle* with Captain Asabel Havens in charge.

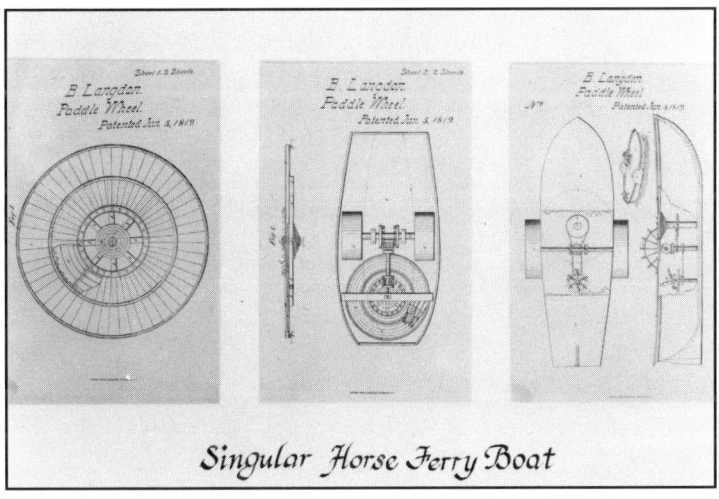

Patent drawings for B. Langdon's horse-powered ferry located by A.P. Beach at the U.S. Patent Office.

Lake Champlain as the Centuries Pass

The Langdon horse ferry was in use in other places besides Lake Champlain. Basil Hall's Travels in 1828 mentions crossing the Hudson in two or three places on a horse ferry. According to his description, they were quite sizeable boats, carrying stage coaches, extra teams and passengers.

During the period 1800-1830, there were at least a dozen ferries operating at different points on Lake Champlain.

In recent years Diesel-powered ferries ply the waters of Lake Champlain, carrying thousands of trucks and automobiles from Vermont to New York.

The history of commercial navigation on Lake Champlain has been well covered in a book published by the Delaware and Hudson Railroad entitled "The Steamboats of Lake Champlain" and by a more recent book by Ralph Nading Hill entitled "Sidewheeler Saga." I will attempt to set down a brief summary of this epoch.

The first vessel to engage in commercial traffic was a small sloop owned and operated by Major Philip Skene of Skenesboro (Whitehall). This boat had a monopoly on the lake shipping until the Revolutionary War when it was seized by General Benedict Arnold, fitted out as a warship,

Detail from a Lake Champlain Steamboat Company broadside, circa 1817.

84

Ferry and Steamboat Service

renamed the *Liberty* and took part in the battle of Valcour Island. At the close of the Revolutionary War, commercial traffic on the lake increased rapidly under the leadership of Gideon King. He kept building sailing vessels until he had a fleet capable of serving all of the ports on the lake from Whitehall to St. Johns. There was great rivalry between these rather sleek sailing vessels and the early scow-type steamboats.

The lake was still the important artery of traffic and more attention was paid to this than road building. This led to the building of many steamers once the mechanical problems were ironed out. From 1809 to 1832, nine steamers were built, one at the mouth of Otter Creek, several in Vergennes, others at Shelburne Harbor. They ranged in size from seventy-five feet to one hundred and fifty feet in length and from one hundred and fifteen to three hundred and forty three tons. Several had short lives, others were operated successfully for many years.

The opening of the first Champlain canal in 1823 did much to increase passenger traffic and shipments on the lake as well as more rapid handling of the mail.

Travel on the lake steamers in 1827 was not too luxurious as is evidenced by Basil Hall's account on September 27, 1827.

"Our route lay along Lake Champlain in a very crowded steamboat, filled with tourists on their return from the North. The machinery was unusually noisy, the boat weak and tremulous and we stopped, backed, and went again, at no fewer than eleven different places, at each of which there was such a racket that it was impossible to get any rest. If a passenger did manage to doze off, under the combined influence of fatigue, and the monotonous sounding of the rumbling wheels, which resembled eight or ten muffled kettle-drums he was sure to be awakened by the quick "tinkle! tinkle!" of the engineer's bell or the sharp voice of the pilot calling out, "Stop her!" or he might be jerked half

85

out of his berth by a sound thump against the dock or wharf.

In the cabin there was suspended a great, staring lamp, trembling and waivering about in a style to make even a sailor giddy. Underneath its rays were stretched out weary passengers, some on mattresses spread on the deck, others on the lockers, or on the bare planks, the very picture of woe, like the field of battle after the din of war has ceased, etc."

In September, 1819, Benjamin Silliman, a Professor at Yale College took a carriage and horses and traveled from Hartford up to Albany and then along through the Saratoga battlefields on which he made interesting observations and finally arrived at Whitehall. Here his carriage and horses were received on board the steamboat *Congress*, which he described as a neat and rapid boat and the only one remaining on the lake. In the channel above Whitehall, he mentions passing the fleets of Macdonough and Downie, which had been brought down there and moored stem to stern after the Battle of Plattsburgh. He says,

"As we passed rapidly, a few seamen showed their heads through the grim portholes from which five years ago the cannon poured fire and death and we caught a glimpse of the decks that were then covered with the mutilated and the slain and deluged with their generous blood. Sparless, black and frowning, these now dismantled ships looked like the coffins of the brave and will remain as long as worms and rot will allow them, sad monuments of the bloody conflict."

Further on he says,

"During our passage of twenty-five miles to Ticonderoga, we had a fine descending sun shining in full strength upon the bold scenery of the lake and that I might enjoy it undisturbed by the bustle of a crowded deck, I took my seat in the carriage where I was protected equally from the fumes of the boat and the chill of the air and could, at my

Ferry and Steamboat Service

leisure, catch every variety of images and all the changes of scenery that were passing before me."

At Ticonderoga he remarks,

"The shadows of the night were descending on the venerable Ticonderoga as we left it and when I looked upon its walls and environs so long and so often clustering with armies, formidable for so great a length of time, and all the apparatus and preparation of war, the object of so many campaigns and battles but now exhibiting only a solitary smoke curling from a stone chimney in its half-fallen barracks with not one animated being in sight, while its massive ruins, the beautiful declivities sloping on all sides to the water, were still and motionless as death."

This trip up the lake was made at night in late September. He arrived at Burlington at three o'clock in the morning, where Professor Silliman left the carriage and horses while he proceeded on to Canada. He mentions that on the trip up, the boat stopped several times at different places on the two shores of the lake to deliver and receive freight and that the captain, being extremely dilatory, said "we were delayed one or two hours at each place."

In 1824 H.G. Spafford published a pocket guide listing fares for travel on Lake Champlain steamers as:

Whitehall to Ticonderoga	24 miles	$1.50
Crown Point	39 "	2.50
Basin Harbor	51 "	3.00
Essex	61 "	3.50
Burlington	75 "	4.00
Port Kent	91 "	4.00
Plattsburgh	99 "	5.00
Chazy	114 "	6.00
Champlain, Rouses Point	126 "	6.50
St. Johns	150 "	8.00

Lake Champlain as the Centuries Pass

There was a stage from Basin Harbor to Vergennes - fare $1.00.

A New York State travel guide in 1843 lists fare from Whitehall to St. Johns at $4.00, a 50% reduction.

The Northern Traveler published in 1826 by A.T. Goodridge supplies a little interesting detail about the travel conditions of the times. He mentions that there is a boat through the northern canal for freight but no part of the boat is expressly used for passengers but that in fine weather, gentlemen may travel very pleasantly for a few miles in the common freight boats. Coming up to Ticonderoga, he mentions that Mr. Pell is the sole proprietor of the whole peninsula of Ticonderoga and has a beautiful home there and fine garden. Speaking of navigation on Lake Champlain, he says, "Great numbers of small schooners navigate these waters and within a few years, numerous canal boats, some of them fitted with masts for schooners for sailing. Annesley's mode of building vessels has lately been adopted here to some extent in which timbers are discarded and the hulls formed of inch boards run in several thicknesses in cross directions."

At Chimney Point he mentions that there is a large public house in a pleasant situation and here is the place to stop if the traveler intends to visit Crown Point, which is opposite across the ferry three-quarters of a mile. Proceeding up the lake to Button Bay, he mentions it as being "Put-In-Bay" on the eastern shore with an island of the same name. A little north the lake appears narrower than it is with a precipice on the left and a small island on the right with three bushes on it which has hence obtained the name of Scotch Bonnet. "Basin Harbor is a stopping place, it is very small with room for only three or four vessels."

Old newspapers of this period expound on the great development of steamboating on the lake. In the 1830s the U. S. Government recognized the need of lighthouses on the lake and a dozen or more were built and maintained for a

88

Ferry and Steamboat Service

century when they were replaced with automatic lights. A newspaper reporter of this era wrote: "Who would have thought that a few years ago the night traffic on the lake would become so heavy that a series of lighthouses would be necessary."

From 1840 to 1850 larger and more luxurious steamers were built. The length increased to 240 feet and the tonnage to 648, the horsepower to 250 and speed to 19 miles an hour.

In 1842 Charles Dickens made the trip from St. Johns to Whitehall on the Str. *Burlington*. His comments on this trip in his American Notes were about the only favorable things said about the United States.

> "There is one American boat—the vessel which carried us on Lake Champlain from St. Johns to Whitehall—which I praise very highly, but no more than it deserves, when I say that it is superior even to that in which we went from Queenstown to Toronto, or to that in which we travelled from the latter place to Kingston, or I have no doubt I may add, to any other in the world. The steamboat which is called the *Burlington*, is a perfect exquisite achievement of neatness, elegance and order. The decks are drawing-rooms; the cabins are boudoirs, choicely furnished and adorned with prints, pictures and musical instruments; every nook and corner of the vessel is a perfect curiosity of graceful comfort and beautiful contrivance. Captain Sherman, her commander, to whose ingenuity and excellent taste these results are solely attributable, has bravely and worthily distinguished himself on more than one trying occasion; not the least among them, in having the moral courage to carry British troops, at a time (during the Canadian rebellion) when no other conveyance was open to them. He and his vessel were held in universal respect, both by his own countrymen and ours; and no man ever enjoyed the popular esteem,

Lake Champlain as the Centuries Pass

who, in his sphere of action, won and wore it better than this gentleman.

By means of this floating palace we were soon in the United States again, and called that evening at Burlington, a pretty town, where we lay an hour or so. We reached Whitehall, where we were to disembark, at six next morning and might have done so earlier, but that these steamboats lie by for some hours in the night, in consequence of the lake becoming very narrow at that part of the journey, and difficult of navigation in the dark. Its width is so contracted at one point, indeed, that they are obliged to warp around by means of a rope."

In 1850, Appleton & Company published what they called the Northern and Eastern Travelers Guide, which is very complete in details of traveling on railroads and steamboats. It says that canal packets and stages leave daily for Troy and Albany from Whitehall and on Lake Champlain, it says several fine steamboats ply between Whitehall and St. Johns, stopping at intermediate places. "The excellent accommodations of these boats, the picturesque scenery on the shores of the lake, crowned by lofty mountains and the interesting locality celebrated in former and the late wars render this excursion delightful."

In a travel book published in 1868, it states that travelers will find Lake Champlain the most directly available route to Canada. Here are fine steamboats on the lake to start their journey, the names being the *Adirondack,* the new and the finest, the *Canada,* the *United States* and the *Montreal.* It goes on to state that the waters abound with bass, pickerel, salmon, trout and other varieties of fish. The scenery of the region is not to be surpassed. At the time this book was published there were only two cities in the State of Vermont, Vergennes, with a population of 1,286 and Burlington with a population of 7,713, which had been incorporated within the previous years.

Ferry and Steamboat Service

The steamboat service continued to thrive under the capable management of the Champlain Transportation Company. In 1871 they built the second steamer, *Vermont*, which was two hundred sixty-two feet long, had a displacement of one thousand one hundred twenty-four tons and cost $200,000.00. This vessel had the honor of carrying Generals Grant, Philip Sheridan and many distinguished people. In July, 1875, one of their large steamers, the *Champlain*, was wrecked on the shore opposite Basin Harbor. The pilot, named Eldridge, who had been taking morphine, dozed off at the wrong time and the large ship tried to climb the mountain. Fortunately, no lives were lost but the steamer was a total loss.

The steamer *Champlain* shown after its ill fated journey onto the New York shoreline. Photo courtesy of Special Collections, University of Vermont Library.

Lake Champlain as the Centuries Pass

The third steamer *Vermont*, built in 1903, was the pride of the fleet and for some thirty years ran a regular schedule from Plattsburgh to Montcalm Landing near Ticonderoga. The ship was licensed to carry nine hundred passengers. It was a pleasant sight to see her passing majestically up and down the lake every day during the summer months.

The *Ticonderoga* was the last of the line of famous steamboats to be built on the lake. Built in 1906, though not as large as the steamer *Vermont*, she had more deck space and was licensed to carry one thousand and thirty-seven passengers. For years the "TI," as she was called, made regular, daily trips from Westport to Plattsburgh. Daily trips on the "TI" were a great source of pleasure to vacationists up and down the shore of the lake; in addition, nearly all of our supplies were brought in by boat during the early years here at Basin Harbor. With the increase of auto traffic, there was a marked decline in the use of steamboats; when the seasonal operation loss reached into six figures, the Transportation Company called a halt. For some years, it was operated as a ferry from Burlington to Port Kent and was finally sold to Captain Alanson Fisher in 1948. He tried vainly to make it pay in the excursion and charter business. In 1950 Ralph Hill came to the rescue of the steamer that was about to be

Steamer *Ticonderoga* [1906-1953] at the dock at Basin Harbor.

Ferry and Steamboat Service

scrapped. Funds were raised by the Burlington Junior Chamber of Commerce to fix up the boat and put it in operation. Finally, it was acquired by Mrs. Watson Webb of Shelburne, who operated it for three years under the personal direction of Ralph Hill. Steamboating on Lake Champlain came to end at the close of the 1953 season. Mrs. Webb then considered the possibility of moving the steamer overland to make it a part of her ever-increasing Shelburne Museum. In November, 1954, this grand old steamer we all had learned to love started on her last journey, this time overland to a final resting place in the famous Shelburne Museum. Thus ended a great era of one hundred and forty-five years of steamboat service down Lake Champlain.

The manner in which the eight hundred ton steamer was moved five miles overland is extremely interesting. It called for a great amount of engineering skill and the expenditure of funds in excess of the original cost of building the steamer.

The boat was piloted to the south end of Shelburne Harbor where some dredging was done to get it as close to the shore as possible. Then a wide bank of earth in the form of a fifteen foot dike was built around the steamer. Hugh pumps were then set to work to bring the water to the top of the dike, thus raising the ship at the same time. A second dike was then built adjoining the end of the first, with walls somewhat higher. Before filling the later two lines of railroad track were placed on ties and a cradle was built of heavy eye-beams on four freight car wheel assemblies suitable for receiving the ship. Then water was pumped in and the steamer floated in over the cradle. With the slow emptying of the dike the ship settled down on the cradle and was ready to be transported. By then the ground was frozen and the two lines of track were laid down, taken up and relaid and heavy winches and tractors were used to haul it very, very slowly towards its destination. It required three months to move the ship across the flat fields. Just before reaching the museum grounds it had to cross the Rutland Railroad tracks, but all was accomplished before the spring thaws came and the ship is now on a permanent cradle where it has come to be a major tourist attraction.

Practically everyone who has resided along the shores of Lake Champlain must have at one time or another taken a trip on the steamer *Ticonderoga* and will have nostalgic memories of the pleasurable rides up and down the lake on this very comfortable steamer. Those who were guests at the club at Basin Harbor will remember particularly in 1950-1953 seasons when the steamer was chartered and everyone was taken on board for a fine sunset ride with a hot meal being served just as the sun was slipping over the Adirondack Mountains to the westward.

10

Recent Events Taking Place in the Champlain Valley

Its Many Attractions

THREE YEARS PREPARATION previous to 1909 by combined commission of the states of Vermont and New York resulted in the staging of the Tercentenary Celebration of the discovery of Lake Champlain by Samuel de Champlain in 1609. The Dominion of Canada was invited to join in the celebration and a very creditable series of events took place. William Howard Taft was president at that time. Charles E. Hughes was Governor of New York, and George H. Prouty was Governor of Vermont. Many distinguished citizens from all over the world took part in the celebration. Monuments to Samuel de Champlain were dedicated at Crown Point and at Plattsburgh. Indians in great numbers were present and pageants were staged at Crown Point, Ticonderoga, Plattsburgh and Burlington, as well as at Isle La Motte and Rouse's Point. The State of New York published a massive fully illustrated book covering every phase of this celebration.

For a great many years there was much discussion about the possibility of building bridges across Lake Champlain which would facilitate travel between the two states. The ferries then operating on the lake provided a very poor form of transportation in the age of fast automobile travel.

LAKE CHAMPLAIN AS THE CENTURIES PASS

During the Tercentennary, huge public ceremonies were held up and down the lake.

Finally, in 1925, a joint commission was appointed by the states of Vermont and New York to study the feasibility of building a bridge between Chimney Point in Vermont and Fort St. Frederic to the New York shore, this being the narrowest point in which a bridge might be built, actually fifteen hundred feet over water from side to side. The bridge itself was twenty-nine hundred feet in length and an overall width of thirty-two feet with twenty-four feet being for the roadway. The center span has a clearance of ninety feet above the lake level. The cost of the bridge was approximately one million dollars of which New York financed sixty percent and Vermont forty percent. The bridge was dedicated on August 26th, 1929. It marked a great epoch in the history of Lake Champlain. Franklin D. Roosevelt, Governor of New York and John E. Weeks, Governor of Vermont participated. It was distinctly understood when these bonds were issued that the bridge would be free after the obligations were paid.

Recent Events in the Champlain Valley

Not only did the tolls from this bridge pay for the bridge sooner than expected but it also helped accumulate funds to build two other bridges at Rouse's Point in Alburg, the third bridge between Swanton and Alburg. The cost of all bridges has now been paid and it is hoped that they may be free to the travelling public, as promised, in the near future.

This year, 1959, plans have been formulated for the 350th Anniversary Festival of the discovery of Lake Champlain. Again New York, Vermont, and Canada are joining in the event and it is hoped that representatives from Holland, France, and England will also be present.

The Lake Champlain Valley has come to be a mecca for travelers from far and wide. There are a number of tourist attractions which continue to be extremely popular. At the lower end of Lake Champlain is Fort Ticonderoga, which has been restored to its former grandeur by the Pell family who, during the past few decades have made it the most complete and historic shrine in the country. In 1955 it celebrated its 200th anniversary. Nearby Fort Hope and the restoration on the top of Mount Defiance also merit a visit and study. Traveling northward one comes to Crown Point and the entrance to the Champlain bridge. Here are the remains of Fort St. Frederic and Fort Amherst and the Champlain monument.

Mention has already been made of Ausable Chasm where many thousand visitors are welcomed each year.

On the Vermont shore the outstanding tourist attraction is found at Shelburne Village Museum. Here a veritable village of structures depicting early Vermont life together with an amazing amount of Americana have been assembled by Mrs. J. Watson Webb. No visit to Vermont is complete without a tour of this fascinating establishment.

Vermont has been endowed with an abundant supply of granite, marble and slate. These provide a source of everlasting building materials which are used to a great extent throughout the nation. Visitors to the Champlain Valley should plan a trip to the granite quarries at Barre and observe the manner in which huge blocks of granite are handled with the greatest of ease. And on the way south the marble exhibits at Proctor, Vermont, will be found equally interesting.

The greatest asset and attraction of the Champlain Valley is in the unchanging scenic beauty of the area. Travelers through the century have been greatly impressed with the grandeur of our lakes and mountain panoramas. It would seem that the member of Burgoyne's staff who wrote so eloquently about the indescribable scenery has summed it up best when he said: "I cannot by any powers of the language do justice to such a scene."

CHRONOLOGY OF IMPORTANT DATES
Pertaining to the Events
Which Took Place in the Champlain Valley

1609	On July 4, Samuel de Champlain discovered the lake that bears his name.
1642	On August 8, Father Joques, Jesuit Priest–captured by Iroquois Indians.
1646	On October 18, Father Joques and companions brutally murdered.
1666	On January 21, M. de Courcelles led a large company of French troops over ice to attack Iroquois Indians. Untold hardships and loss of life.
1666	On July 26, Fort St. Anne built on Isle La Motte.
1666	On September 28, M. de Teacy led force of 1200 troops down lake in 300 bateaux and canoes for attack on Mohawk villages. The largest force seen on lake up to that time. Many distinguished soldiers in this expedition.
1684	On November 4, a grant of land made to Peter Schuyler, Robert Livingston.
1687	Governor Donogan proposes to build a fort at Corlaer's Lake 150 miles north of Albany at Chimney Point.
1688	French consider plans to build fort at Crown Point.
1689	On June 7, Count de Frontenac appointed Governor of New France.
1690	On January 15, Frontenac organized party of French and Indians that came down the lake and dealt crushing blow to English settlements at Schenectady.
1690	March 26, Captain Jacobus de Narm led force to set up defensive outpost at Chimney Point. The first English occupation of shores of Lake Champlain.

99

1690	April 1, Captain Abram Schuyler led force to mouth of Otter Creek where they set up camp.
1690	On August 13, Captain John Schuyler traveled up the lake with troops and Indians.
1690	On August 23, Schuyler forces dealt severe blow to French settlement at La Prairie burning all the buildings.
1690	On August 30, passed Basin Harbor in triumph on way to Crown Point.
1691	In mid-June passed up the lake and again defeated Frenchforces.
1693	In mid-winter, French force passed down the lake on ice to attack Mohawk villages. Captured prisoners and suffered extreme hardships; returned to Canada.
1696	September 3, Godfrey Dellius, a Dutch minister at Albany, secured a grant to land on Lake Champlain extending to Rock Reggio, Split Rock (afterwards revoked).
1698	Attempts made without avail to secure peace treaty and exchange of prisoners. Godfrey Dellius acted as envoy.
1709	On June 29, John Schuyler led band and Indians to Otter Creek and encountered French forces under command of M. de Ramezay.
1713	On April 13, the treaty of Utrecht was signed ending hostilities between England and France. Established Split Rock as southern boundary of New France.
1720	French owners explore area around Basin Harbor and named "Bassin" Harbor appears on their charts.
1730	On October 15, Governor Beaubariois proposed the construction of a fort at Crown Point.
1731	On May 8, construction of Fort Frederic started at Crown Point; was completed September 22.

1733	In month of April, twelve or more seigniories were granted on the shores of Lake Champlain.
1734	On July 7, Sieur Contrecoeur received a grant of shore property including Basin Harbor.
1737	On June 13, Louis-Joseph Rocbert secured a grant of land north of Split Rock including the Boquet River.
1743	On April 20, Gilles Hocquart, Governor of New France, received a large grant of land including Chimney Point, site of Vergennes and Basin Harbor, from King of France.
1749	On July 2, Peter Kalm, noted Swedish traveler, travels from Whitehall to Canada and reports on the fort and countryside.
1749	The first sawmill in the Champlain Valley was built on Missisquoi River by Rene-Nicolas Levasseur, who did shipbuilding for the French forces.
1750	On July 30, Fort Frederic reported to have 20 cannon, a four-story stone citadel with walls ten feet thick. There were 14 farms near the fort.
1754	English plan to destroy Fort Frederic. French and Indian War starts.
1755	Construction started on Fort Carillon (Ticonderoga) under the direction of de Lotbiniere.
1756	On July 8, the first naval engagement between the English and French took place off the shores of Charlotte. Captain Robert Rogers commanded the English bateaux.
1757	Stone walls of fort substituted for original timber structure; some 2,000 men worked on fortification.
1757	On June 30, General Montcalm arrived at Fort Carillon with large force transported in 200 boats and canoes.
1758	On July 8, French forces under Montcalm defeated English army under General Abercrombie.

1759	On July 15, French settlements along the lake being mostly abandoned.
1759	On July 31, General Jeffrey Amherst in command of English and colonial troops, moved up to attack Fort Carillon. On July 31, French forces abandon Fort Carillon, largely due to failure of French government to support the campaign. On July 31, French blow up Fort Frederic, thus ending a period of 28 years under the French.
1759	Early in August, Captain Loring came to Crown Point to start construction of fleet for Amherst to use in attacking French fleet.
1759	In August, plans to fortify Crown Point with building of Fort Amherst got under way. Ten million dollars spent on this fort.
1759	On August 16, the French fleet of four ships was reported cruising on the north part of the lake.
1759	On September 1, the French launch 16-gun ship at Isle aux Noix.
1759	On October 11, Amherst's fleet sailed up the lake to attack. On October 14 French fleet sunk in about five fathoms of water near New York shore above Plattsburgh.
1759	On October 21, Amherst's fleet returned to Crown Point for winter.
1760	Major Robert Rogers headed an expedition to attack French forces at the north end of the lake.
1762	On June 24, Benjamin Ferris and others secure Charter for Township of Ferrisburg.
1762-1775	Colonial settlers came in to take over sites evacuated by French soldiers who fought in area.
1763	On April 7, M. de Lotbiniere purchased grant of Gilles Hocquart for 9000 livres, about $1800.00.

1769	Col. Reid secured title from Albany to a tract of land 4 miles wide either side of Otter Creek and established a mill there with Donald McIntosh in charge.
1775	On May 10th Ethan Allen and a band of Green Mountain Boys captured Fort Ticonderoga.
1776	On October 11th met the British fleet in battle at Valcour Island.
1777	During the month of June General Burgoyne came down from Canada with the largest military force ever seen on Lake Champlain.
1814	On September 11th, Commodore Thomas McDonough defeated the British fleet at Plattsburgh.
1929	On August 26th, the bridge connecting Fort St. Frederic and Chimney Point was dedicated.

BIBLIOGRAPHY

Bailey, John H. <u>Bulletin of Champlain Valley Archaeological Society</u>, Vol. 1, 1939.

Bourne, Annie Nettleton, translator. <u>Voyages of Champlain, Narrated by Himself</u>. Allerton Book Co., 1904.

Champlain Transportation Company. <u>The Steamboats of Lake Champlain</u>. Albany: The Champlain Transportation Company, 1930.

Costain, Thomas Bertram. <u>The White and the Gold.</u> Toronto: Doubleday, 1954.

Crockett, Walter H. <u>A History of Lake Champlain.</u> Burlington, Vt: McAuliffe Paper Co., 1937.

Dunbar, Seymour. <u>A History of Travel in America.</u> Indianapolis: Bobbs-Merrill, 1915.

Fenton, Carroll Lane. <u>Our Amazing Earth.</u> New York: Doubleday, Doran & Co., 1938.

Fiske, John. <u>New France and New England.</u> Boston and New York: Houghton, Mifflin & Co., 1902.

Hemenway, A.M. <u>The Vermont Historical Gazetteer.</u> Burlington, Vt: A.M. Hemenway, 1868-91.

Hill, Ralph Nading. <u>Sidewheeler Saga, A Chronicle of Steamboating.</u> New York: Rinehart, 1953.

Hill, William H. <u>Old Fort Edward Before 1800.</u> Fort Edward, NY: William H. Hill, 1929.

Macdonough, Rodney. <u>Life of Commodore Thomas Macdonough, U.S. Navy.</u> Boston, Ma: The Fort Hill Press, S. Usher, 1909.

Moore, Ruth E. <u>The Earth We Live On.</u> New York: Knopf, 1956.

Pell, S.H.P. <u>Fort Ticonderoga, A Short History.</u> Ticonderoga, N.Y.: Fort Ticonderoga Museum, 1935.

Richards, Horace Gardiner. <u>Record of the Rocks.</u> Ronald Press Co., 1953.

Rogers, Robert. Journals of Major Robert Rogers. Albany: J. Munsell, 1883.

Royce, Caroline Halstead Barton. Bessboro: A History of Westport, Essex County, New York. (n.p., 1902)

Shuler, Ellis William. Rocks and Rivers. New York: Ronald Press Co., 1945.

Silliman, Benjamin. A Journal of Travels in England, Holland, and Scotland, and of Two Passages Over the Atlantic. New Haven: S. Converse, 1820.

Smith, H.P. History of Addison County Vermont. Syracuse: D. Mason & Co., 1886.

Tebbel, John. The Battle for North America. Garden City, NY: Doubleday, 1948.

Thompson, Daniel P. Green Mountain Boys. Chicago: Rand McNally, 1912.

Van Doren, Carl. Secret History of the American Revolution. New York: The Viking Press, 1941.

Vermont Historical Society Quarterly, 1938.

Watson, Winslow Cossoul. Pioneer History of the Champlain Valley. Albany: J. Munsell, 1863.

Williams, Samuel. The Natural and Civil History of Vermont. Burlington, Vt: SamuelWilliams, 1809.

Winsor, Justin, ed. Narrative and Critical History of America. Boston and New York: Houghton, Mifflin & Co., 1884-89.

Wissler, Clark. Indians of the United States. Garden City, NY: Doubleday, 1940.

AFTERWORD

A.P. BEACH CLOSES HIS BOOK, published in 1959, by taking a look at recent events in the Champlain Valley during his time. In this afterword, written in 1993, I would like to do the same.

Since the publication of A.P.'s book, much has changed in our understanding of the lake's history. With the retirement of the *SS Ticonderoga* in the early 1950's, the lake became something of a backwater. No longer were the once-flourishing commercial harbors used by merchant traders, but rather by a relatively few (by today's standards) recreational sailors. The historic statues erected in 1909 during the "Tercentenary," the valley-wide celebration of the lake's history, became part of the background scenery. Awareness of the lake as an historic body faded in most people's consciousness.

Like many things that run in cycles, however, so does our sense of historical appreciation. If the 1960's and 70's saw a decline in this awareness, the 80's and 90's have seen it renewed. In the earlier decades, waterfront traffic declined, ferry service was reduced to only four seasonal crossings, and the lake's historic images began to fade. Public school curricula deemphasized local history in favor of world history, and to a young girl or boy from the town of Addison, Arnold's Bay was a place with good fishing, not the site of naval action during the American Revolution.

Fortunately, the pendulum is now swinging back to a greater appreciation of Lake Champlain's historic role in regional, national and international affairs. One reason is the documentation of a vast collection of shipwrecks beneath the waters of the lake. Each discovery causes us to ask: "Who owned this boat?" "Who built it?" "What were the events surrounding its sinking, and what does this tell us about what life was like back then?" Each vessel has its own

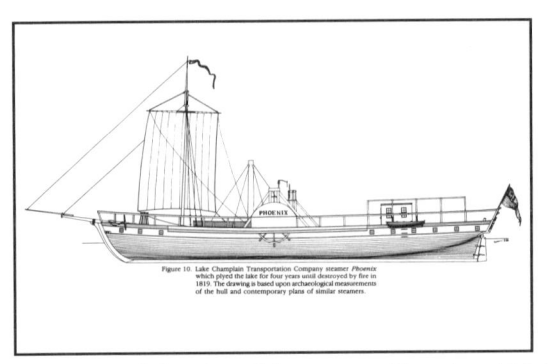

Reconstructed drawing of the steamer *Phoenix*, which burned on a trip from Burlington to Plattsburgh on September 5, 1819. The *Phoenix* has been located and studied and today she is one of Vermont's Underwater Historic Preserve sites. Drawing by Kevin Crisman.

story to tell, and its own cast of characters. These vessels are often the only link we have with the past, and the more we find out, the more curious we are.

Another reason for increased awareness of the lake as an historic body is the expansion, since A.P.'s time, of historic sites open to the public. Saratoga Battlefield has been designated a National Historic Park, and Skenesboro, now Whitehall, where Revolutionary forces rushed to build a naval fleet, is now a New York State Urban Cultural Park, complete with an interpretive visitor center. The venerable Fort Ticonderoga still dominates the valley, providing visitors with an unparalleled reflection of the vast 18th century armies and armadas which once fought for control of the lake.

Directly across the lake from Fort Ticonderoga is a Vermont State Historic Site, Mount Independence. This site is rich in archaeological information still being uncovered. North at the next strategic narrows stands Crown Point, now a New York historic site, and across the lake is Chimney Point, a recently-opened Vermont site focusing on Native American and French occupation.

*MAP of
LAKE CHAMPLAIN
depicting
FERRY CROSSINGS
and
HISTORIC SITES*

Chambly
St. John

Isle aux Noix

Richelieu River

Plattsburgh
Clinton County
Historical Museum

**Grand Isle/
Cumberland Head Ferry**

**Burlington/
Port Kent Ferry**
Ausable Chasm

Burlington
Ethan Allen Homestead
Fleming Museum

Shelburne Museum

Shelburne Farms

**Charlotte/
Essex, NY
Ferry**

Elizabethtown
Adirondack Center

Basin Harbor
Lake Champlain
Maritime Museum

Blue Mt. Lake
Adirondack Museum

Chimney Point

Crown Point

Middlebury
Vermont Folklife Center
Sheldon Museum

Fort Ticonderoga

Ticonderoga Ferry

Mt. Independence

Whitehall
Skenesboro Museum

109

Saratoga
Battlefield

Ten miles north of Chimney Point is A.P. Beach's beloved Basin Harbor, the resort which has been in his family for over 100 years (now under the fourth generation of Beach family management). It is also the location of the Lake Champlain Maritime Museum, which was established in 1986 as a central location to preserve and interpret the heritage of the Champlain Valley. In many ways, the Museum is an outgrowth of A.P. Beach's love of the lake, passed down to the next generations and fueled by new studies of the lake's vast submerged cultural resources. This collection of shipwrecks, perhaps the richest in North America, is providing new insights to this history as well as stimulating debate about their long-term preservation.

Up the coast, a new Shelburne Farms, now open to the public, is a gathering place for environmental and agricultural information and education. Its neighbor, the Shelburne Museum, offers one of the best national collections of American folk art. It is also home to the retired *S.S. Ticonderoga* and the Colchester Reef Lighthouse, both reminders of an earlier era on Lake Champlain.

North of Shelburne is Burlington, home to the Ethan Allen Homestead, a new museum which interprets the life and times of one of Vermont's premier settlers. Northward on the New York side is the Clinton County Historical Museum in Plattsburgh. This recently-relocated museum provides great regional perspective with a strong focus on Macdonough's victory at the 1814 Battle of Plattsburgh Bay. Further north on the Richelieu River are the Parcs Canada sites of Fort Lennox of Isle aux Noix and Chambly. Both sites are connected to the lake by the Richelieu waterway, which accounts for the shared history.

Interspersed throughout the valley are dozens more exceptional historical museums and great natural wonders. The Adirondack Center in Elizabethtown and the Adirondack Museum at Blue Mountain Lake, along with the Vermont

Folklife Center and the Sheldon Museum in Middlebury, all have rich cultural perspectives to share with residents and visitors alike. Ausable Chasm, the Adirondacks, the Green Mountains and the Champlain Islands provide magnificent natural backdrops for exploring the Valley.

While the dozens of lake ferry crossings have been reduced to four, each surviving crossing has been in operation for over two hundred years and has endured radically changing times. The Shoreham-Ticonderoga ferry still uses a cable to guide it across the lake. The Charlotte ferry, once propelled by six horses, brings travelers to and from Essex, New York, a historic hamlet whose architecture directly reflects the lake's 19th century past. On the summer Burlington-Port Kent run, travelers can cross the lake on the *Adirondack*, the oldest running ferry in the United States, and possibly the world. If they take the northern Grand Isle-Cumberland Head crossing, they can travel on the lake's newest ferry, the recently-christened *Vermont IV*.

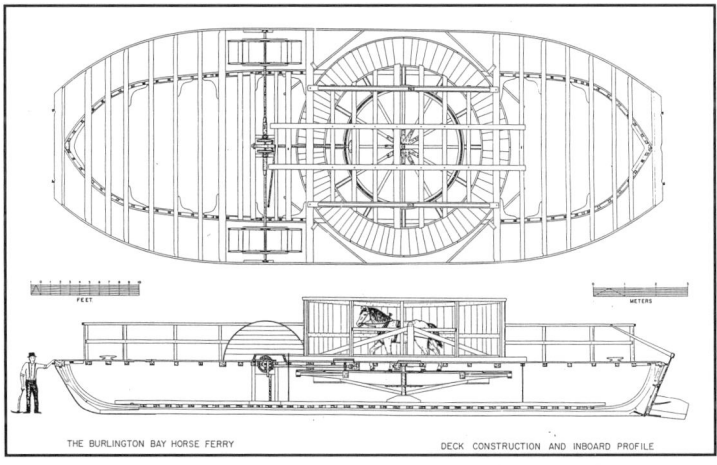

Plans for the horse-powered ferry located and studied in Burlington Harbor. The Burlington Bay Horse-Ferry is one of the Vermont Underwater Historic Preserve sites. Drawing by Kevin Crisman.

Much of the history presented by A.P. Beach was new information at the time, which later researchers have since built upon. Take, for example, A.P.'s discovery of the horse ferry material at the National Archives, and his descriptions of these relatively short-lived craft. In the past ten years one of these craft has actually been located under fifty feet of water in Burlington Bay. The origins of the particular boat remain a mystery, but the two horse-powered "Langdon"-designed vessel is currently the only surviving example of this type of watercraft. The horse ferry has been the subject of a multi-year underwater archaeological documentation and is one of several sites included in Vermont's Underwater Historic Preserve system.

Over the past fifteen years, Maritime Museum researchers have had the unexpected privilege of locating and studying "in-situ" a variety of underwater sites so rich it would have surprised even A.P. Beach. Just about all historic times are represented: Native American dugout canoes; French and British colonial naval craft; American and British Revolutionary-time ships; remnants from the submerged "Great Bridge" which spanned Fort Ticonderoga and Mount Independence; American and British War of 1812 ships; and commercial vessels of all kinds, including the *Phoenix*, the

Many historic vessels have been located and raised from Lake Champlain. Unfortunately, like the *Duke of Cumberland* (circa 1759) above, being raised in 1909, most of these vessels have decayed to extinction.

oldest surviving steamboat hull in the world. As exceptional as these discoveries are, it is important to realize that as of this writing, we are only beginning to scratch the surface of the size and diversity of this collection.

Aiding our efforts is a recent technological leap in the way underwater sites are located and studied. In the 19th century, historic vessels had to be seen from the surface "at low water" to be found, at which point they were often raised. Using side-sonar and other modern equipment, researchers can now locate sites in the deepest regions of the lake. Many shipwrecks still lie undiscovered in the lake's waters, and new advances in

The reproduction Revolutionary War vessel *Philadelphia II* being rowed out of Basin Harbor just after launching on August 18, 1991.

electronic technology have the potential to reveal all of the lake's previously hidden secrets. Although the submerged vessels are on the lake's bottom for a variety of reasons—some were abandoned, some sank in battle, some sank in peacetime maritime disasters—they all enrich our knowledge about the past.

Refinement of underwater archaeological documentation techniques has enabled researchers to produce reports, books, documentaries and exhibits about these underwater sites and share them with schoolchildren and the public. The Maritime Museum has recently experimented with a new interpretive process made possible by these improved techniques. To satisfy public interest about what these ships really looked like, the Museum has begun to build full-sized, working replicas of historic vessels, which allow people to "see what it looked like" without jeopardizing the original. Once the replica is completed, the Museum has an operational exhibit which can be utilized for a variety of interpretive programs.

One could argue that no body of water in North America has played such an integral role in our country's development from an Indian homeland to a European colony to a free nation, as has Lake Champlain. Those who live and travel in the Champlain Valley see that history reflected in the region's historic sites and museums, architecture, the now-rare fuel barges coming up through the canal, and the operating ferries with their crews of present-day Lake Champlain mariners.

In writing this book, A.P. Beach reminds us that in studying clues from the past, we discover insights into the present. It is a worthy pursuit; this generation bears the responsibility not only for preserving our historic sites, but also for instilling an appreciation for them in our youth. Only then can we ensure the historical resources available to us today, will remain to tell their story for future generations.

Much has happened in the 35 years since A.P. Beach first published this book, but one thing is certain: he and the other fine lake historians who have passed to our generation the baton of knowledge would be pleased to see it passed on again, today.

    Arthur B. Cohn
    February 14, 1993

The new *Philadelphia II* underway on Lake Champlain.

printed on recycled paper

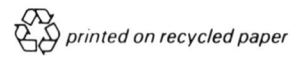